RECOLLECTIONS

THE DETROIT YEARS

THE MOTOWN SOUND BY THE PEOPLE WHO MADE IT

JACK RYAN

EDITED BY

THOMAS J. SAUNDERS

PUBLISHERS

GLENDOWER MEDIA, LLC

WHITMORE LAKE - TORONTO

2012

RECOLLECTIONS

THE MOTOWN SOUND BY THE PEOPLE WHO MADE IT

SECOND EDITION

TJS/GM

GDM

ISBN 9780914303046

www.glendowermedia.com

Introduction to the 30th Anniversary Edition

It has been over 30 years since this book was completed on Motown Records. In that time many things have changed. Berry Gordy has sold the company to Universal Media and the Motown Studios which produced so many hits is now a museum.

The biggest change of all is the tragic loss of so many of the labels' stars, artists we had come to know like our own family members. In their place, groups have surfaced that have no connection with the latter day versions of the original groups.

Time and artists may change but the one thing that will never change for the true Motown fan is "The Sound".

The Motown label was called "The Sound Of Young America". It may no longer be the sound for young America but it will always be the music that makes the Motown fan feel young.

FORMER MOTOWN ACTS NO LONGER WITH US

Eddie Kendricks	Earl Van Dyke
David Ruffin	Eddie Willis
Melvin Franklin	Counsil Gay
Cholly Atkins	Beans Bowels
Maurice King	Marv Johnson
Levi Stubbs	Mary Wells
Renaldo Benson	Taylor Cox
Ron White	Flo Ballard
Edward Patten	Pervis Jackson
Jr. Walker	Billy Henderson
Pistol Allen	C. P. Spencer
Michael Jackson	

INTRODUCTION

It was quite exciting to grow up in the Detroit area during the sixties when the Motown era was hitting its heights.

For the first time in memory, black music was being bought, played and enjoyed by all types of audiences. This marketing phenomenon was no accident. Berry Gordy, Jr. had decided to create a sound which would appeal to all listeners. The end result was known as "The Motown Sound" and if you were around in the sixties, it was virtually impossible to turn on a radio without hearing a Motown recording.

This book is dedicated to "The Motown Sound" and the people who produced it. You made my life a lot more enjoyable with the music you created.

1982

TABLE OF CONTENTS

ACKNOWLEDGEMENTS

I would like to publicly thank the following individuals without whose help I never would have been able to complete this book.

Eddie Kendricks	Pat Harrington	Willie Tyler
Melvin Franklin	Kim Weston	Eddie Willis
Otis Williams	Council Gay	Sylvia Moy
David Ruffin	William Guest	Joe Billingslea
Levi Stubbs	Thomas Bowles	Sylvester Potts
Obie Benson	Maurice King	Dick Purtan
Duke Fakir	Cholly Atkins	Robin Seymour
Lawrence Payton	Marv Johnson	Tom Sherman
Mary Wilson	Martha Reeves	Marc Avery
Stevie Wonder	Ros Ashford-Holmes	Tom Shannon
Bobby Rogers	Lois Reeves-Jackson	Larry London
Claudette Robinson	Katherine Anderson	Marjorie DeBenedetto
Smokey Robinson	Gladys Horton	Gary Lichtman
Ron White	Mary Wells	Hank O'Neil
Gladys Knight	Taylor Cox	Mildred Goodwin
Edward Patten	Pervis Jackson	Alan Sklar
Bubba Knight	Billy Henderson	Tom Myers
Jr. Walker	Bobby Smith	Fox Theater
Richard Allen	Henry Fambrough	C&G Publishing

Earl Van Dyke

Penni Stephens

Todd Norton

Paul Meyers

Lana Yates

Liz Shimunic

Susie Keats

Rita Finn

Joseph LaFleur

Michael Newman

Betty Ann Jones

Coletta Perry

Tim Nixon

Annie Capps

Doyle Robinson

Rick Rueckert

Julie Rueckert

Elizabeth Savage

Charles Perry

Jill Foltz

Marla Braciszewski

A special thanks goes to my beautiful wife, Kathy Ryan, and to my publisher Thomas J. Saunders. Without their constant belief in me and this project, none of this book would have been possible.

MAURICE KING

1. Artist Development

Directly across from HITSVILLE stood Artist Development on Grand Boulevard

Did you ever wonder why the Motown acts looked so good on stage? Did you ever wonder why their choreography was so perfect, or why they sounded much like their recordings when you saw them in a concert?

The answer lies within a small group of professionals formed by Motown to create a department known as Artist Development.

I never gave it a thought until I heard so much about Maurice King, Johnny Allen, Cholly "Pops" Atkins, and Maxine Powell of Artist Development during my research for this book, and learned it was the first such department of its kind connected with a record company.

The names I mentioned earlier are not exactly household names as far as Motown goes, but anyone connected with the company will tell you that these individuals had as much to do with its success as anyone.

Artist Development came about in the early 1960's. Berry Gordy and his brother-in-law, Harvey Fuqua, who was an executive at Motown, noticed that although their acts were starting to get hit records, they lacked polish and finesse. Harvey Fuqua, a former entertainer himself with Harvey and The Moonglows, urged Berry Gordy to set up a studio in a vacant area in the Motown Studios, a place where acts could rehearse regularly. That being accomplished, Fuqua set about contacting his former choreographer, Cholly Atkins, who lived in New York.

Cholly Atkins

Cholly Atkins' background as a dancer went back a long way. He was half of the famous dance team of Coles and Atkins. They had appeared on Broadway, been in movies and toured with such luminaries as Count Basie and Duke Ellington. Atkins had retired as a performer and now was working as a choreographer in New York. Fuqua reasoned that with Cholly's professional background he could polish up the raw talent Motown possessed.

Atkins told me about his decision to come to Motown. "Harvey had contacted me several times over a two year period about joining the Motown staff. I was in New York with my own studio, working with various acts in the area. I was doing pretty well, but Harvey came up with an offer that was too good to pass up. I had complete control of choreography for all of the Motown groups. I figured that I would enjoy this type of a challenge, so I cast my lot with Motown. It was one of the best decisions of my life. "

For Atkins, the challenge of working with this tremendous group of raw talent was the ultimate test of his ability. Each of the twenty-plus Motown acts presented him with a unique situation. "I tried to fit the choreography to the individual or group. I would study them to see what their abilities were. From there I would question them to see where they wanted their careers to go. I wanted to find out if they wanted to stay a Rhythm & Blues act or whether they wanted to become a nightclub act. From this type of close scrutiny I was able to put together the routines that would best showcase their talents."

Cole and Atkins

The company encouraged as many of their acts as possible to learn cross-over material. Berry Gordy foresaw his acts working all of the major nightclubs in America. He knew that in order to achieve his lofty goals, his acts would have to appeal not only to black audiences but to all segments of the population. He had seen the success that his friend Jackie Wilson was enjoying throughout the world. His appeal had no color barrier, and he wanted this type of success for his Motown acts.

Surprising as it may seem, it wasn't hard to get the artists to go along with the strenuous work set before them. In most cases, they had been doing their own choreography, so any professional help was greatly appreciated. Cholly Atkins explained that some acts were easier to work with than others. "The Temptations and Gladys Knight and The Pips were my prize pupils. They adapted so well to whatever I asked them to do. All of the groups worked hard for me and most of them adapted well to what I designed for them. "

Many groups presented unique problems for Cholly but no challenge was too big for him. The Contours, for example, were quite large men, like football players. Cholly designed choreography which they could adapt to their style to so they would look fluid in their movements. The Supremes, the top stars with the company, came to Cholly as tomboys. Cholly evaluated them and saw that they had the potential to become superstars. Berry Gordy encouraged everyone at Artist Development to do everything they could to bring these three tomboys along. The result of their work is obvious.

To the casual observer the stage presence and choreography were a delight to the eye, but Cholly explained that it was more than just an overnight job to get a group ready for the stage. "We would work for up to 6 hours a day, 6 days a week, up to 8 weeks. This schedule was nonstop and if for any reason they weren't ready, I would go out on the road with them. I would even work with them between shows to ensure the proper message was carried through the choreography."

Diana Ross gave Cholly Atkins the ultimate compliment at a Las Vegas performance when she introduced him to the audience and gave him credit for teaching her the proper delivery and moves which helped her get to where she is today. Not bad for an old hoofer.

UPDATE: In 1989, Atkins received a Tony Award for choreographing the Broadway show "Black and Blue." Diagnosed with pancreatic cancer in March 2003, Atkins died of the cancer several weeks later on April 19, 2003 in Las Vegas, Nevada at age 89.

Motown Choreographer CHOLLY ATKINS

Maurice King

Maurice King is not a name that most people would associate with Motown Records, but all of the singers he worked with over the years remembered him fondly.

5

Mr. King was in charge of voice and music for the Artist Development Department of Motown Records. He not only helped the singers with their vocals and arrangements, but he was one of the most sought-after musical directors at Motown. He conducted for such talents as The Supremes, Marvin Gaye, The Miracles, and Gladys Knight and The Pips.

Berry Gordy was no stranger to Maurice King when he offered him a position at Motown. He had known Maurice from The Flame Show Bar where King was musical director for eleven years. Gordy's sisters worked at The Flame and Berry was a frequent visitor, coming in after work to see the artists who would be performing under King's leadership. King himself, after his departure from The Flame, was working with several of Gordy's top acts in his private studio. The Temptations, Mary Wells, and The Supremes were students of his at the time Berry approached him to become the head of the music department of Artist Development. King remembered the day Berry made him that offer. "I was working with some of his acts already and he explained it might be a lot easier if I joined his staff and worked regularly with all of the Motown acts. I liked the idea of an artist development department, and being able to have control of the musical end of it was quite an exciting aspect."

The Flame Show Bar, center of black entertainment in Detroit

Berry never interfered with his department heads. They were given a job to do and were expected to do it. Gordy had a great plan, in which all of his acts would be able to play the finest showplaces in the world. Preparing his acts was the responsibility of Artist Development.

Marvin Gaye was one of the hardest workers at Motown. He was being groomed to become a nightclub artist and the pace that was set for him at Artist Development was brutal. King recalls some of the work that went into Gaye's development. "We had Marvin working up to 12 hours a day on routines that ranged from tap dancing to work with a top hat and cane. We put a show together for him that would appeal to the audiences at the Copa in New York. That was a different audience than Marvin was used to working, so it was a real challenge to get him ready. But ready he was, and the work was worth it. "

King saw a lot of Marvin Gaye because he was his musical director during his concerts, but he also conducted for Motown's top group, The Supremes. "The Supremes broke the ice for all our groups. They were the first on The Ed Sullivan

Show, the first in The Copa and the first into Las Vegas. We all knew if they made it, then all of our acts would have an easier time of it. The Supremes never let us down."

It was not a mistake that The Supremes and the groups that followed them made such a big hit in these major show spots. They were all taken on the road to five different clubs around the country to work the kinks out of their show, such as the Broadway shows do before they open in New York. It was the job of Artist Development to see that the problems were all worked out prior to a big opening night.

Maurice also worked as a trouble shooter and conductor when any of the Motown acts performed on any of the major television shows such as Ed Sullivan Show, Dean Martin Show, or The Hollywood Palace. These shows proved to be quite a thrill for King. "We would always come in a day before the show to work with the various orchestras on our material. I got along quite well with such orchestras as Les Brown, Nelson Riddle, and The Ed Sullivan Orchestra. When they would find out that a Motown act would be on the show, they would always inquire if I was going to be the conductor. I had a very good working relationship with these people, and I am very proud of that. "

As in most cases, all good things must come to an end, and for Maurice King and Artist Development, the end came with Motown's move to California. Not wanting to leave his home in Detroit, Maurice chose to stay behind. He was in big demand as a musical director, and worked with Gladys Knight and The Pips for several years. At the present time, he is musical director for the Spinners.(1982)

King had his own ideas on Motown's departure from Detroit. "I knew that they wanted to get into motion pictures badly and to do that, they would have to move to California. Many of the old Motown acts stayed in Detroit, and I did work for them, but I still missed the family atmosphere at Motown."

Almost every Motown act from that magical era left with a little bit of Maurice King and Artist Development in them. Whenever you watch someone who had worked with Motown and noticed that something special in the way they perform, you'll know why.

I asked Mr. King if he could sum up his feelings on his involvement with Motown. His answer was as professional as the man himself. "I tried to teach the performers honesty, integrity, and sincerity in their approach to the business. If they learned that, then they learned a lot. As for my Motown memories, whenever I hear a medley of my arrangements that I did for the various groups, then I know my contribution will last as long as the songs are performed."

UPDATE: Maurice wed his longtime friend Nellie Foreman just a few months before his own death on December 18, 1992. "Maurice died because he just got tired of living. He just stopped eating," claims Clarence Jr.. "He did it his way. He did everything his way."
His funeral was packed with people he'd worked with, helped, or supported in some type of musical activity. They'd come to pay their last respects to the King of Detroit music.

Maxine Powell

Maxine Powell was another member of Artist Development that did quite a bit of background work at Motown. Her job was to work with the female groups on make-up, grooming, poise, and personal hygiene.

Maxine Powell came to Motown through a friendship with the Gordy family. She had worked as a finishing instructor with Berry's sisters. Her work was so highly thought of that when Berry was putting together the Artist Development Department, Maxine was contacted to work with the girls.

When it came to working on poise and grace, Miss Powell had her work cut out for her. Most of the girls at Motown were in need of Miss Powell's services. Many of the girls came to Motown as sort of tomboys. Coupled with the tomboy problem was the fact that most of the girls were teenagers and hadn't developed the natural grace and poise that comes with the maturing process. They were young and from poor backgrounds where finishing schools were out of the question. Maxine taught them the finer points of make-up, poise, diction, and dress. It was important for all of the Motown groups to look attractive and well-groomed, on stage and off. Miss Powell was also a big help in picking out the gowns that the girls wore. It was imperative that the girls look feminine and attractive for the various clubs and shows they would be working. She was instrumental in choosing the first gowns that The Supremes wore.

Despite the obstacles mentioned, Maxine and the girls worked very hard on their poise and appearance. It wasn't long before the ladies of Motown were the epitome of elegance both on and off the stage.

The makeovers on the groups proved to be invaluable to Berry Gordy's grand scheme of things. He wanted his acts to work the best clubs and with the help of Maxine Powell, he was able to accomplish many of his goals.

Now you know why the female groups at Motown always looked their best. It certainly was not an accident. Few things were left to chance at Motown. Nothing was left to chance at Artist Development.

2. The Andantes

The Andantes were a group of three ladies whose voices were on more hit records than any other Motown group. They were part of the regular cadre of background singers who were part of the Motown staff.

These ladies were heard on virtually every record that used female background singers. They never pushed for a solo career because they were quite content to stay on the sidelines and, quite honestly, they lacked the stage presence to be really big stars.

The Andantes were a group you may have never heard of, but you have heard them many times without knowing it.

MEMBERS:

Jackie Hicks
Marlene Barrow
Louvain Demps

UPDATE:

As part of the Ivan Levine's Motorcity Records project in the late '80s and early '90s, The Andantes were signed to the label and once again provided a service in recording backing vocals to former Motown artists. By this time, Pat Lewis had joined Jackie, Marlene and Louvain (from 1989-1992). The women had not worked together in a number of years, although all had been busy providing demo and backing vocals for numerous artists on various labels. Motorcity Records boss Ian Levine also recorded several songs with The Andantes, issuing a new single, "Lightning Never Strikes

Twice", which featured Louvain Demps on lead vocals. Most other songs recorded by the group at Motorcity had Pat Lewis on lead vocals.

3. J. J. Barnes

Another of the artists Motown acquired when they purchased Golden World Records was J. J. Barnes. Barnes had enjoyed quite success at Ric-Tic and Groovesville Records before he went to Golden World. The song for which he is best known was a tune entitled "It's Alright".

J. J. did have a connection with Motown, for Martha and The Vandellas were his backup singers when they were known as The Vells. J. J. enjoyed his greatest popularity in his hometown of Detroit, where he was in constant demand at various clubs and nightspots. He really never did much recording with Motown because the company felt he had his biggest success behind him.

J. J. did appear regularly with the "Motor Town Revue". He was a good showman and this quality was greatly appreciated by the Motown officials. J. J. Barnes was not a big name in the history of Motown, but he served them well during his stay with the company.

UPDATE: His biggest hit single came in 1967 with "Baby Please Come Back Home", which, like many of his records, he co-wrote. The song reached #9 on the American *Billboard* R & B Chart . However, subsequent singles on a variety of labels, including covers of "Black Ivory" at Today/Perception Records, failed to repeat the success.

4. Chris Clark

Chris Clark

Chris Clark may not have been a big success at Motown, but it wasn't for lack of effort. Chris happened to be a major project of Berry Gordy's and he wanted desperately to make her a big star at Motown.

Chris, you see, was one of the very few white acts Motown employed, and Gordy wanted to show the world he could do more than sell black artists. Chris had a lot of talent, but unfortunately, she didn't have a strong voice and she lacked stage presence. Very often she would be drowned out by the backup singers working with her.

In 1967, Clark released an album, called *Soul Sounds* on the Motown label. The album featured twelve songs, including a rare Motown ballad called "If You Should Walk Away" (Berry Gordy, Jr.) which was slated for release as a single, but never was. Chris Clark recorded one more album for Motown on its newly created rock label, Weed , called *C.C. Rides Again* (1969), but the album failed commercially. It remains the only album ever released on the Weed label.

Undaunted, Berry Gordy had all of his best people work with Chris and a lot of material was released, but nothing ever sold very well.

Chris was a mainstay of the Motor Town Revue and stayed on with Motown serving in many capacities after she retired from show business.

UPDATE: Clark co-wrote the screenplay for the 1972 Diana Ross vehicle *" Lady Sings The Blues"* , for which she was nominated for an Academy Award. She later became an executive for Motown Productions' film and television division in Los Angeles.

In 1982 she married Academy Award -winning screenwriter and novelist Ernest Tidyman. He died of a perforated ulcer in 1984.

In recent years, Clark has become an art photographer and has exhibited her work mainly to art dealers and at a few galleries. She also performs onstage occasionally in clubs in the United States and in Europe. She currently lives in Santa Rosa, California.

Chris Clark 2000

5. The Contours

In the late 50's many singing groups were formed in and around the Detroit area.

With the success of such local talents as The Falcons and Jackie Wilson, starry-eyed young men would form various groups, hoping for that one big shot at stardom. That's how it started for The Contours. Billy Hoggs, the group's leader, got together with four of his friends: Sylvester Potts, Hubert Johnson, Billy Gordon, and Joe Billingslea. Together they formed a group called The Blenders. Joe Billingslea and Billy Gordon had been singing with a group called The Majestics, and when the opportunity arose to join the new group, they jumped at it.

The Blenders enjoyed modest success in various Detroit night-spots, but the shot at a record contract was eluding them. They eventually got an appointment with Wes Higgins of Flick-Contour Records. They brought along a tune titled "Come On And Be Mine", which Higgins liked very much indeed. Unfortunately for The Blenders, he didn't care for them personally. He already had a group called The Falcons who were doing quite well, and he felt they didn't need any competition from within the company.

Joe Billingslea explains how the group changed their name upon leaving Higgins's office. "When we were walking out of the office, I noticed the name Contour on the office door. I felt the name suited us so we took a vote, and from that day on, we were called The Contours."

Eventually The Contours came to the attention of Berry Gordy at Motown Records. An audition was arranged, but to the group's dismay, Gordy wasn't very impressed. He encouraged them to keep working on their act and come back and see him at a later date. They were quite discouraged when they went to visit Jackie Wilson, who was Hubert Johnson's cousin.

That afternoon remains etched in Joe Billingslea's mind. "We went over to Jackie's house to see what kind of advice he could give us. He asked us to sing some of our material for him and he seemed quite impressed. He got up from his chair and went into the other room to make a call. We had no idea he was on the phone with Berry Gordy. After he got off the phone he told us that Berry wanted to see us in his office immediately. When we got there he had a seven year contract waiting for us to sign." That was a decision that proved to be wise for both Gordy and The Contours.

It was a Gordy written composition that proved to be the biggest hit for The Contours. It was also the fastest climbing hit Motown had ever released. The song was titled "Do You Love Me" and within three weeks of its release it was number two on the charts.

From there The Contours continued their succession of hits with such tunes as "First I Look At The Purse", "Shake, Sherry, Shake", "Can You Do It", and "Can You Jerk Like Me". It was a great time to be part of the Motown family.

Council Gay, another member of the early Contours, has these Motown memories: "We had a certain unity within the group and the company. Every group at Motown was putting out hits and the company's reputation was spreading far and wide. Acts from all over the world wanted to record with Motown, so if you were part of that mystique, you took great pride in being with Motown."

Being with Motown also had certain drawbacks. If you had a popular record, you could be on the road touring for up to six months. The Contours were no different. When "Do You Love Me" was at the top of the charts, the group only came off the road to record another record, then they would be back on the road. Berry Gordy was great believer in letting the public see his stars.

Like all good things, the success that The Contours achieved came to an end. After several unsuccessful releases, the writers and producers started gearing their material to other acts. This was not an uncommon occurrence in the record business. As Council Gay explains, "If you were a writer and you were trying to make a name for yourself, who would you write your material for? Certainly not a group who had several failures in a row. It's purely a matter of going with a winner. There were so many male groups at Motown that the competition was very keen. So if your records weren't selling, you were moved to the end of the line when material was written. I feel personally that if it hadn't been for Laucye Whitfield, who liked our music, we probably wouldn't have done as well as we did."

Another reason for The Contours' fall from popularity was their choice to stay in the rhythm- and- blues vein. Motown was encouraging their performers to explore more crossover material. Nightclubs were the next world Berry Gordy wanted to conquer and to become a good nightclub act, they would have to be able to perform standard material.

The Contours

While most acts were encouraged to visit the company's Artist Development Department regularly (in fact it was required for most acts), The Contours were told that besides the very basics of onstage behavior, there wasn't very much they could be helped with. This was not meant to be a putdown of The Contours, it was simply the truth. They had organized their own choreography which served their up-tempo songs very well. Their stage act was one of the most energetic and acrobatic of the Motown galaxy of stars. As stated earlier, Berry Gordy was trying to move into nightclubs, and cart-wheels, back flips and splits were frowned upon.

Early in 1964 the original Contours broke up. Many reasons contributed to the breakup, including pay differences with Motown. Coupled with their increasing displeasure with the type of material they were recording and quite a few problems internally, it was difficult to maintain the continuity that a group such as The Contours must have. Motown tried to replace members and went through many singers attempting to keep the group going.
From that point there was quite a turnover in the group with Hugh Davis, Council Gay, Jerry Green, Dennis Edwards, Sylvester Potts, and Joe Stubbs all either coming or leaving the group. When the Contours original seven year contract expired, the group disbanded.

The memories that were left are bittersweet for Joe Billingslea, "We were given a great opportunity at Motown. We enjoyed great success and we really enjoyed the family atmosphere that was at the company at that time. As the company grew, that atmosphere changed and the company became so large that I don't think they were able to give the proper attention to all the groups they had at the time."

A photo of The CONTOURS
as they appear today
L to R:
Martin Vaughan, Arthur Henson,
C. Autry Hatcher, Joe Billingslea,
Sylvester Potts

The Contours 1982

At this time (1982) The Contours have regrouped and are working around the Detroit area. The group is currently made up of Joe Billingslea, Council Gay, Martin Vaughn, Arthur Henderson, and C. Autry Hatcher. They all have various jobs outside the music business and they are treating their re-entry into show business with guarded optimism. Joe Billingslea summed up life as a member of The Contours. "Being a member of a group that was famous has only kept the desire to perform alive in me all these years. All I ever wanted to do was sing. I probably never really left show business and I probably never will."

UPDATE: In the early 1970s, Joe Billingslea resurrected the group with himself, Council Gay, Arthur Hinson, Martin Upshire and C. Autry Hatcher as its members, and began performing at local clubs around Detroit. During the seventies and early eighties, the group's popularity increased and they began playing dates throughout the U.S. and even some international dates. In 1984, Charles Davis replaced Hinson and a week later, Potts rejoined the group, replacing Gay. In 1987, Hatcher left the group and Arthur Hinson returned. In 1988, Darrell Nunlee was added when Martin Upshire left. The same year, "Do You Love Me" was prominently featured in the film "Dirty Dancing". In 1988, a reissue of "Do You Love Me" sent the song back to the Billboard pop charts for eight weeks, peaking at number eleven. The movie and the record spawned a 1988 "Dirty Dancing Concert Tour" followed by a new recording contract for Ian Levine's Motorcity Records. The group recorded two albums *"Flashback"* and *"Revenge"* although the latter was not released even though the songs came out on a later compilation.

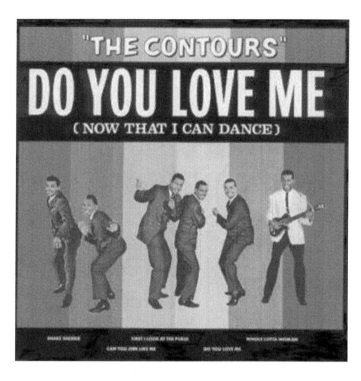

In 2004, Sylvester Potts left to form his own group with the four members (Leroy Seabrooks, Kim Green, Tony Womack and Darell Nunlee) of a local Detroit group named Upscale, which immediately began performing as "The Contours". Billingslea sued and Potts countersued, each claiming the rights to the name. These suits were resolved in an out-of-court settlement which provided for the existence of both groups to be identified as "The Contours with Joe Billingslea" and "The Contours featuring Sylvester Potts," respectively. Seabrooks has since left the Potts group, making it a quartet. In 2006, the Contours with Joe Billingslea filled the vacant bass singing spot created by Potts' departure with Odell Jones. Both groups are currently performing.

Founding member Billingslea continues to perform with his group, "The Contours with Joe Billingslea", which is among the acts featured in a DVD released by Motown in January 2007 called "Motown: The Early Years," on many Public Broadcasting System specials. In March 2010, the Contours were inducted into the Doo-Wop Hall of Fame. The induction show featured a performance by The Contours with Joe Billingslea. Original member Hoggs left The Contours in 1964 to become a minister. Today he is retired and lives in Mt. Pleasant, Michigan. In 2005, Hoggs made his first and only appearance since 1964, singing with Billingslea and The Contours for the taping of "Motown: The Early Years". Johnson committed suicide in Detroit on July 11, 1981. Gordon died in 1999, and Fair followed in December 2004. Mid 1960s member, Joe Stubbs - brother of Levi Stubbs - died on February 5, 1998. Huey Davis (pictured on the Do You Love Me album cover, but never officially a member of the Contours) died on February 23, 2000, at his home in Detroit.

Potts continues to perform with his version of the Contours. They can be seen in the 'Ultimate Doo Wop' series of concerts that travel around the United States each year.

In 1964, The Contours recorded a second album for Motown entitled *The Contours: Can You Dance* (Gordy 910). It featured the chart hits, "Can You Do It, Can You Jerk Like Me, "That Day When She Needed Me", and nine other tracks, including The Marvelettes' hit, "Danger: Heartbreak Dead Ahead". For hazy and not fully understood reasons, this album was unreleased by Motown, but in April, 2011, the album's original tracks, along with fourteen unreleased original Contours 1960s Motown recordings, and new 2011 interviews with original Contours members Joe Billingslea and Sylvester Potts, was released as part of the CD compilation collection, *Dance With The Contours* on the import label, Kent Records, under legal license from, and with the full approval of, the owners of the Motown catalogue.

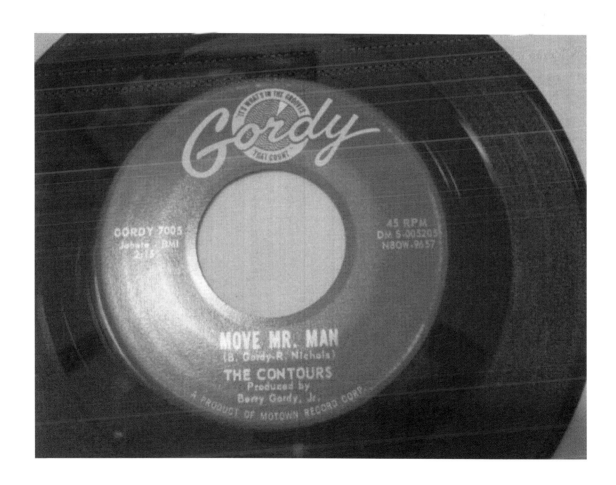

6. The Elgins

Surprisingly enough, The Elgins arrived at Motown having enjoyed two very big hit records at another record company. Founding members Robert Fleming, Norbert McClean, and Johnny Dawson recorded prior to their Motown days as The Sensations, The Five Emeralds, and The Downbeats before adding Saundra Edwards (Mallett) and adopting the name "The Elgins" in 1964.

When they were known as The Sensations, their hits were "Music, Music, Music "and "Let Me In ".

They came to Motown hoping to enjoy the success that other groups were having. Unfortunately, it didn't turn out that way. After changing their name to The Elgins, which was a name The Temptations had once used in their early days, the group did quite a bit of studio background work until the right type of material was found for them.

Motown officials were enthusiastic about The Elgins but the company had quite a few bigger acts at the time that demanded attention, so The Elgins were relegated to opening act status until they had a hit record. The two songs that were the group's biggest successes, "Heaven Must Have Sent You" and "Darling Baby", were dwarfed by hits from other major Motown artists.

During the remainder of their stay at Motown, The Elgins worked various tours as an opening act, hoping to have a hit song with Motown. I suppose they often wondered why they ever signed with Motown, after having been successful before they arrived at the Detroit Studio A on West Grand Blvd.

THE FOUR TOPS

An early publicity shot of
FOUR TOPS

7. The Four Tops

THE FOUR TOPS

When Duke Fakir, Levi Stubbs, Obie Benson and Lawrence Payton got together and formed The Four Tops in the mid-fifties, they probably had no idea that nearly three decades later, they would still be going strong. Founded in Detroit, Michigan as The Four Aims, lead singer Levi Stubbs (born Levi Stubbles, a cousin of Jackie Wilson and brother of The Falcons' Joe Stubbs), and groupmates Abdul "Duke" Fakir, Renaldo "Obie" Benson and Lawrence Payton remained together for over four decades, having gone from 1953 until 1997 without a single change in personnel.

The Four Tops started out much like many singing groups of the era. They sought stardom, fame and wealth, and figured one sure-fire way to achieve their goals was by forming a singing group.

Unlike many groups, The Four Tops hung onto their dream for nearly ten years before they gained the popularity they have enjoyed since the mid-sixties. As Lawrence Payton related to me," We started out singing in talent shows as teenagers. Before long, we were appearing at clubs and lounges that we weren't old enough to walk into. This exposure gave us a taste of the spotlight and we got really turned on by it. Right then and there, I think we all realized that this was what we wanted to do as a career." As stated previously, quite a few groups had the taste for stardom, but one thing lacking from their acts was perseverance. As a result, many very talented groups bit the dust. One of the secrets to The Four Tops' success was that they were all good friends and were working toward a common goal.

Duke Fakir put it very well when he explained how the group made it through ten very hard years. "We made a commitment to ourselves that we would stick it out no matter how hard it got. It helped us that we were great friends and we all had the same goal in mind. We wanted to make The Four Tops work, no matter how long it took."

It took plenty to keep The Four Tops together during those lean years, but in the long run, it helped them to develop their style--a style that would serve them well in the ensuing years.

The group eventually moved into the recording studio with various companies, hoping to find that elusive hit record. They had very little success with records, but in the interim they were becoming very accomplished nightclub performers. They were working at many top night spots in the resort circuits of Las Vegas, Miami Beach and the Catskills. The club work kept them going financially, but one thing was missing--a hit record. A hit record was a calling card to the national exposure they sorely needed.

Levi Stubbs explained that they were given support from some very influential artists. "We knew Jackie Wilson quite well, and he was a constant source of encouragement.

He assured us that if we stuck it out, something big would happen for us. My brother Joe belonged to a group called The Falcons and they had a hit with a tune called "So Fine". It did quite well and that gave us some hope that our turn would come."

The break The Four Tops were looking for came along in the form of Berry Gordy. The Four Tops knew Gordy from The Flame Show Bar, a nightspot in Detroit where many of the top black performers worked at the time. Gordy's family had the cigarette and photo concessions at the club, and Berry would stop in religiously to scout talent for his newly formed Motown Record Company.

Obie Benson tells of the group's early relationship with Berry Gordy. "We had known Berry through our friendship with Jackie Wilson. Berry had written several hit songs for Jackie, including "Lonely Teardrops". Berry suggested that we come over and talk about recording with Motown. We figured that being a local operation, we had nothing to lose, so we agreed to give it a shot." As it turned out, going with Motown didn't turn out to be any bonanza for The Four Tops. Gordy had given priority to certain groups at the company and was concentrating on getting their careers off the ground before he launched any new projects. During their early Motown years, the Four Tops recorded jazz standards for the company's Workshop label

The Four Tops were left in the recording studio as backup singers. As it turned out, the exposure helped the group grow with the company. "We sang on most of Motown's biggest hits," said Duke Fakir. "We developed some great friendships with other performers at Motown. Everyone pulled for each other-- the arrangers, the musicians, and the other singers. It was new and exciting for us all to be in on the ground floor of a musical revolution." Everyone seemed to be putting out records, but the group was assured that when some material came along that was right for them, it would be a big hit. The songwriting team of Holland, Dozier, and Holland got together on a song for The Four Tops. It was titled "Baby I Need your Loving" and as promised, the record put The Four Tops in the spotlight. The time they had been waiting for was at hand. As happens in show business, The Four Tops were an overnight success, at least in the public's eyes. Behind them lay ten years of perfecting their craft.

The Four Tops, along with Motown, were about to embark on one of the most successful chapters in the music industry. Over the next seven years, The Four Tops were to amass thirteen top ten hits, and Motown was to grow to staggering heights. There was a reason for the meteoric rise of "The Motown Sound", as it was now termed. For the first time in memory, white listeners were turning on to "The Motown Sound". Lawrence Payton tells the story: "When we would go out to perform, the audience was predominantly white. We thought it was a bit strange, but in the final analysis, it was the white audience that was creating the success we were all enjoying." Indeed, it was the white audiences that picked up on the fresh "Motown Sound", and at one time during the sixties, turned Motown Records into the top recording company. In the early days of rock and roll, many black artists who had hit records were quite disappointed to see their music recorded by white artists and released to white audiences without ever mentioning that they had recorded the song.

"Berry had the foresight to see that his sound would cross over these color lines if it was handled properly," remarked Payton.

Levi Stubbs explained to me, "We all spent a lot of time working at the Motown Artist Development Department, refining our acts so that we would fit into the full-scale plans that Berry had for the company. He saw his performers as top paid nightclub, television, and movie attractions. Because we had worked the nightclub circuit before, we were expected to be a big part of his plans."

It was a magical time in The Four Tops' career. They would go around the world playing to sold out houses and standing ovations. They were very popular in England, as were most of the Motown acts. Princess Margaret was one of their biggest fans.

Obie Benson recalls those English memories, "We got to meet Princess Margaret after one of our shows. We were quite surprised to find out she was a fan. All in all, those trips to England were quite exciting. When we would arrive at the London Airport, there would be thousands of kids waiting to get a look at us. It was a bit like the popularity English groups were experiencing in the United States."

As the sixties were drawing to a close, Motown was growing by leaps and bounds. Caught up in the growth was the close family atmosphere everyone had shared in the early days of the company. When the Four Tops contract ran out in 1971, they were searching for more of a commitment from Motown concerning their career. Times had changed at Motown. At one time they had been able to go in and talk to Berry Gordy, but there were other channels to go through now. Quite honestly it peeved the Four Tops to think that they had to stand in line to see their boss. Duke Fakir put it quite simply. "We worked very hard trying to work out a contract with Motown, but it wasn't to be. It broke our hearts to leave Motown, but we felt we weren't getting the attention we needed."

The Four Tops told me that to each man this was the biggest disappointment in their careers. There seemed to be no hard feelings on either side. After all, The Four Tops and Motown had been good to each other's growth. The Four Tops were part of the concrete that built Motown Records and would keep intact for some time to come.

Lawrence Payton summed up the Four Tops chapter with Motown in a very honest manner. "It seems that with all the egos to contend with at Motown, it was inevitable that people would have their feelings hurt and leave the company. I think we were all very lucky to have been a part of music history, The Motown Era."

Whenever people are working together on something that is very special, they probably do not realize how special it is until it is over. I'm sure any performer who worked with Motown during that special time would agree. The Four Tops do.

UPDATE: Since the 1980s, the Four Tops have recorded for, at various times, Motown, Casablanca Records and Arista Records. Today Universal Music Group controls the rights to their entire post-1963 catalog (through various mergers and acquisitions), as well as their 1956 single, "Could It Be You".

Four Tops in concert 2007

A change of line-up was finally forced upon the group when Lawrence Payton died on June 20, 1997. The band initially continued as a three-piece unit calling themselves The Tops,[1] before Theo Peoples (formerly of The Temptations) was recruited as the new fourth member. Peoples eventually took over the role of lead singer when Stubbs suffered a stroke in 2000 with his position assumed by Ronnie McNeir . On July 1, 2005, Benson died of lung cancer, with Payton's son Roquel Payton replacing him. Levi Stubbs died on October 17, 2008. Fakir, McNeir, Payton, and Harold "Spike" Bonhart , who replaced Peoples in 2011, are still performing together as The Four Tops. Fakir is now the only surviving founding member of the original group.

The group was inducted into the Rock and Roll Hall of Fame in 1990, and into the Vocal Group Hall of Fame in 1999. In 2004, Rolling Stone Magazine ranked them #79 on their list of the 100 Greatest Artists of All Time. In 2005, The Four Tops were inducted into the Michigan Rock and Roll Legends Hall of Fame. In 2009, the group's first big hit, "Baby I Need Your Loving", was voted a Legendary Michigan Song.

After similar releases in the Motown "Definitive DVD" series on The Miracles, The Temptations , The Supremes , and Marvin Gaye , The Four Tops' Motown Definitive DVD, "Reach Out," was finally released on November 11, 2008.

The Four Tops received *The Grammy Lifetime Achievement Award* as part of the 51st Annual Grammy Awards.

APOLLO

253 W. 125th STREET   HARLEM, NEW YORK

Tuesday, Sept. 27th
STARTS AT 9:00 PM

THE FOUR TOPS

" Reach Out I'll Be There "

"Baby I Need Your Loving"   "Ask The Lonely"

WITH

· Johnny Tabot and De Thangs ·

DANCE ★ CONCERT ★ SHOW

8. Marvin Gaye

At left Marvin Gaye with three backup singers who later became Motown Super-stars, Martha and the Vandellas
Photo Courtesy R.ALLEN

Marvin Gaye was born the son of a minister in Washington D.C., and his first singing experience came in his father's choir.

When Marvin entered high school, he again joined the choir, where he broadened his musical horizons from religious to contemporary music. He would more than likely have followed in his father's footsteps, if it weren't for a recurring dream he used to have while he was a high school student. "I would have this dream where I would be singing to a mass of humanity," relates Marvin. "They would all be listening very intently while I sang, so I took this dream to be some sort of sign that I should be a singer."

After a hitch in the Air Force, Marvin began singing with a group known as The Rainbows. It was at this time that Marvin met the legendary Bo Diddley. Bo took Marvin under his wing and helped him organize a new singing group called "The Marquis", which realized some modest success.

The Rainbows with Marvin Gaye on the right

Harvey Fuqua, who had a very successful group known as Harvey and The Moonglows, auditioned The Marquis for a recording contract and became their tutor.

Eventually, Harvey Fuqua went to work with Motown Records in Detroit. When Motown needed some musicians, Fuqua recalled Marvin's talents on the drums and sent for him. Initially, Marvin Gaye worked as a musician at Motown, playing drums for a variety of recordings. It wasn't until Berry Gordy overheard Marvin playing a tune on the piano one day that Gaye began his recording career.

Marvin singing a soulful ballad
Photo Courtesy T. COX

Marvin recalls that day in the recording studio. "I was just fooling around with a song titled "Stubborn Kind of Fella" on the piano, and Berry came over to me and said I should work on the tune. He said he liked it, and I could record it. That was my first solo recording for Motown." Joining Marvin on the record were three young women who would have quite a successful Motown career in their own right: Martha and The Vandellas.

Marvin followed up his first song with "Pride and Joy" a tune he personally wrote about his wife Anna, who was Berry Gordy's sister. With these two hits under his belt, Marvin began rolling out hits like cars off the Detroit assembly lines. Such hits as "How Sweet it Is To Be Loved", "You're A Wonderful One", "I'll Be Doggone', and "Can I Get A Witness", coupled with Marvin's good looks made him a very popular figure at Motown in the 60's.

*Marvin Gaye first joined Motown as a
drummer
Photo Courtesy EARL VAN DYKE*

It must be said, however, that Marvin always seemed a bit uncomfortable on stage. The immense stardom that was his for the taking always seemed to be a burden to Gaye. Berry Gordy, always the innovator, saw a way for Marvin to enjoy his stardom as well as popularize a new Motown concept—the duet.

Marvin told me, "I was against the project at first, but once we got started, the idea became a lot more appealing. My first duet was with Mary Wells, then Kim Weston, and finally Tammi Terrell, where the best work was done." To say that Tammi and Marvin were successful would be a huge understatement. In 1967 with the release of "Ain't No Mountain High Enough", there began a string of five top ten hits. Included were "Your Precious Love", Ain't Nothing Like The Real Thing" and "You're All I Need To Get By".

"You're All I Need To Get By"

There seemed to be no end in sight to the success of Marvin and Tammi. As their popularity soared so did their record sales, until one fateful night in Cleveland, Ohio. As Tammi came on stage to do her act prior to Marvin coming out to do his show, she felt a bit faint. She continued with her show until she started to collapse. At that point Marvin rushed on stage and Tammi collapsed into his arms. Although Marvin was quite shaken, he continued with the show, thinking Tammi was suffering from exhaustion. It was later discovered that she was suffering from a brain tumor. After several operations to correct the problem, Tammi died. Tammi's death devastated Marvin. The two had been great friends, and for the next two years, Gaye wouldn't tour and rarely entered the recording studio. Motown Executives began to wonder if Marvin would ever recover. But in fact, Marvin Gaye was entering a new phase of his career. Marvin recalls what affected his attitude towards his music. "In 1969 or 1970, I began to reevaluate my whole concept of what I wanted my music to say. I was very much affected by the letters by my brother was sending me from Viet Nam, as well as the social situation here at home. I realized that I had to put my own fantasies behind me if I wanted to write songs that would reach the souls of people. I wanted them to take a look at what was happening in the world."

In 1971, Marvin released an album that was not well received by the Motown brass. *What's Going On.* It was quite different from any of his other material that Motown was used to. As a matter of fact, Motown didn't want to release the album at all. Berry Gordy prevented Gaye from releasing the song, fearing a backlash against the singer's image as a sex symbol and openly telling him and others that the song "was the worst record I ever heard". Gaye, however, refused to record anything that was Motown's or Gordy's version of him. He later said that recording the song and its parent album "led to semi-violent disagreements between Berry and myself, politically speaking." Eventually the song was released with little promotion on January 17, 1971. The song soon shot up the charts topping the R&B chart for five weeks. Eventually selling more than two million copies, an album was requested, and Gaye again defied Gordy by producing an album featuring lengthy singles that talked of other issues such as poverty, taxes, drug abuse and pollution. Released on May 21, 1971, the *What's Going On* album instantly became a million-seller crossing him over to young white rock audiences while also maintaining his strong R&B fan base. Because of its lyrical content and its mixture of funk, jazz classical and Latin soul arrangements which departed from the then famous "Motown Sound" , it became one of Motown's first autonomous works, without help of Motown's staff producers.

Marvin told Motown to release the album or he would do no more for them. Much to their surprise, the album was a huge success, as were the two singles, "What's Going On" and "Inner City Blues" which was released as singles from the album. Motown had failed to realize that the country was going through some interesting changes and Marvin spoke of those changes as his public listened. He followed up with such hits as "Mercy, Mercy, Me" and "Trouble Man". "Trouble Man" was a triumph of sorts for Marvin, for it marked the first time he had scored a motion picture.

Marvin Gaye and Stevie Wonder during a
Motown recording session
Photo Courtesy R. Ashford Holmes

Marvin's professional life was going great guns, but his personal life was in great torment. He and Anna, his wife, went through a very messy divorce following Motown's move to California. Marvin, who had always been a rebel of sorts, eventually left the country rather than pay what he thought were unfair taxes. He left Motown Records and signed with Columbia, severing a 20 year relationship. People who know and love Marvin Gaye hope this new chapter in his life will mean a return to the music we have all loved for so long. (1982)

UPDATE: After signing with CBS' Columbia Records division in 1982, Gaye worked on what became the *Midnight Love* album. Gaye reconnected with Harvey Fuqua while recording the album and Fuqua served as a production adviser on the album, which was released in October 1982. The parent single, "Sexual Healing", was released to receptive audiences globally, reaching number-one in Canada, New Zealand and the US R&B singles chart, while becoming a top ten U.S. pop hit and hitting the top ten in three other selected countries. The single became the fastest-selling and fastest-rising single in five years on the R&B chart staying at number-one for a record-setting ten weeks.

"Sexual Healing" won Gaye his first two Grammy Awards including Best Male Vocal Performance, in February 1983, and also won Gaye an American Music Award for Favorite Soul Single.   In February 1983, Gaye performed the National Anthem at the NBA All Star Game.   In March 1983, he gave his final performance in front of his old mentor Berry Gordy for *Motown 25*, performing "What's Going On". He then embarked on a U.S. tour to support his album. The tour, ending in August 1983, was plagued by Gaye's returning drug addictions and bouts with depression.

When the tour ended, he attempted to isolate himself by moving into his parents' house in Los Angeles. As documented in the PBS "American Masters" 2008 exposé, several witnesses claimed Marvin's mental and physical condition

spiraled out of control. People posing as friends and other hangers on tormented him continually. He threatened to commit suicide several times after bitter arguments with his father. Early in the morning of April 1, 1984,

London Palladium 1977

Gaye's father fatally shot him when Gaye intervened in an argument between his parents over misplaced business documents. The gun had been given to his father by Marvin Jr. four months previously. Marvin Gaye would have celebrated his 45th birthday the next day. Doctors discovered Marvin Sr. had a brain tumor but he was deemed fit for trial and was sentenced to five years of probation after pleading guilty to voluntary manslaughter. Charges of first-degree murder were dropped when it was revealed that Gaye had beaten Marvin Sr. before the killing. Spending his final years in a retirement home, he died in 1998. In 1987, Marvin Gaye Jr. was posthumously inducted into the Rock and Roll Hall of Fame. He was also given a star on the Hollywood Walk of Fame in 1990. In 2005, Marvin Gaye Jr. was admitted into the Michigan Rock and Roll Legends Hall of Fame. In 2007, two of Gaye's most important recordings, "I Heard It Through The Grapevine" and "What's Going On", were voted Legendary Michigan Songs.

In 2008, Rolling Stone ranked Gaye at number six on its list of The Greatest Singers of All Time, and ranked at number eighteen on "100 Greatest Artists of All Time."

BERRY GORDY

Detroit Genius Berry Gordy

9. Berry Gordy

In 1959, a young man named Berry Gordy was working for Ford Motor Company in Detroit, Michigan, but his dream was to become a record producer. His creativity went much deeper than the assembly line and he believed with the right break, his dream would become a reality. His family provided him with a loan from the family bank which would set him on the first step of a rather fantastic journey into the world of entertainment.

Before the journey would end, he would be the owner of the number one recording company in the world: Motown Records. Berry Gordy had dabbled in the music business for several years prior to founding Motown. He had written a couple of songs for his friend Jackie Wilson, which Wilson turned into big hits-- "Reet Petite" and "Lonely Teardrops".

These modest successes gave Gordy the incentive he needed to move forward with his dream. He knew that the talent existed in the City of Detroit, and he was determined to uncover it. Two of his first discoveries were Smokey Robinson and his group, The Miracles, and a young man named Marv Johnson. On January 21, 1959, "Come To

Me" by Marv Johnson was issued as Tamla 101. United Artists Records picked up "Come To Me" for national distribution.

Gordy sold several of The Miracles' tunes to Chess Records with limited success, but he struck pay dirt with a Marv Johnson tune he leased to United Artists. That tune was titled "You've Got What It Takes" and it moved into the top five on the national charts. The money brought in from this tune provided some much needed working capital.

Berry Gordy and Motown brass at 20 Grand, scene of recruiting for Motown

Eventually Gordy tired of having the other companies release his product, and with the help of his sister Gwen and her husband, Harvey Fuqua, his dream of having total control of a record became a reality. Harvey and Gwen owned Anna Records in Detroit and they co-produced a song Gordy wrote himself. The song was titled "Money" and turned out to be the very first hit record Motown had. The singer, Barrett Strong, stayed on with Motown as a producer for many years.

Gordy opened the Motown Studios in a building located at 2648 West Grand Boulevard in Detroit. He and his sister eventually merged their record companies and renamed the building "Hitsville U.S.A". Gordy was not known for cultivating white artists, although some were signed, such as Nick and The Jaguars, Mike and The Modifiers, Chris Clark , Rare Earth , The Valadiers, Debbie Dean and Connie Haines.

As I stated earlier, Berry Gordy's concept of entertainment was very creative. One of the things Gordy pledged was to attract all types of listeners to his music, not just black audiences. His feeling was that entertainment should know no color lines, and to that end, he saw that his artists would appeal to all types of listeners. Gordy's gift for identifying and bringing together musical talent, along with the careful management of his artists' public image, made Motown initially a major national and then an international success.

It was at this time that the term "Soul Music" became a catch phrase for black-oriented music. One of the reasons for the term was Motown's immense popularity among whites. It no longer could be considered "Race Music". On each Motown record was the inscription, "The Sound of Young America," which was exactly the sound Gordy was searching for. It is this sound and phrase that marks the genius of Berry Gordy.

In the early days of Motown, the company always managed to put out several hit records a year which provided the funding to keep the business afloat. In 1961, Motown released "Shop Around" by The Miracles and "Please Mr. Postman" by The Marvelettes, which provided Motown with their first Gold Record and number one hit respectively.

Both groups were home-grown, and before long Motown was attracting all the untapped talent the Detroit area had to offer. All of the pieces were beginning to fall into place for Motown as Gordy assembled a top-notch staff of writers, musicians and performers, along with the best producers.

Gordy, who married and divorced three times, has eight children: Hazel Joy, Berry Gordy IV, Terry James, Sherry, Kennedy , Kerry, Rhonda Ross, and Stefan (Redfoo of LMFOA). His publishing company, Jobete, was named after his three oldest children, **Jo**y, **Be**rry and **Te**rry.

With first wife Thelma Coleman he has children Hazel Joy, Berry Gordy IV, and Terry James. They married in 1953 and divorced in 1959.

In Spring 1960 he married second wife Raymona Mayberry Liles. Their son Kerry — born the previous year on June 25, 1959—is a music executive. They divorced in 1964.

Kennedy Gordy, born March 15, 1964 is the son of Berry Gordy and then mistress/girlfriend Margaret Norton. Kennedy is better known as the Motown musician Rockwell .

Rhonda Ross Kendrick, born August 13, 1971 is the daughter of Gordy and the most successful female Motown artist, Diana Ross, with whom he had a relationship from 1965 to 1970.

Stefan Kendal Gordy, born September 3, 1975, is Gordy's son with Nancy Leiviska. He is also known as Redfoo of the group LMFOA . Skyler Gordy, born August 23, 1986, a grandson of Berry, is the other member of the group, and he uses the alias SkyBlu.

Sherry is his daughter by Jeena Jackson.

After dating for eight years, Berry married Grace Eaton on July 17, 1990. They divorced three years later in 1993

You can see for yourself how Berry Gordy's master plan became more than just a dream. This book is dedicated to all of the people who made that dream a reality.

UPDATE: On March 20, 2009 Gordy was in Hollywood to pay tribute to his first group and first million-selling act, The Miracles, when the members received a star on the Hollywood Walk of Fame . Speaking in tribute to the group, Gordy said "Without The Miracles, Motown would not be the Motown it is today."

He gave a speech during the Michael Jackson memorial service in Los Angeles on July 7, 2009. Gordy suggested that 'The King of Pop' was perhaps not the best description for Jackson in light of his achievements, and chose instead "the greatest entertainer that has ever lived."

On May 15, 2011 it was announced that Gordy was developing a Broadway musical about the Motown music label. The show is said to be an account of events of the 60's and how they shaped the creation of the iconic label. Gordy hopes to use the musical to clear the sullied name of Motown Records and clear up any misconceptions regarding the label's demise.

B.G.E. "MOTOR TOWN SPECIAL" SHOW

I T I N E R A R Y

*****

DATE		CITY & STATE	PLACE OF ENGAGEMENT
Friday	November 2, 1962	Boston, Massachusettes	Boston Arena
Saturday	November 3, 1962	New Haven, Connecticut	New Haven Arena
Sunday	November 4, 1962	Buffalo, New York	Memorial Auditorium
Monday	November 5, 1962	Raliegh, North Carolina	Raliegh City Auditorium
Tuesday	November 6, 1962	Charleston, South Carolina	County Hall
Wednesday	November 7, 1962	Augusta, Georgia	Country Club
Thursday	November 8, 1962	Savannah, Georgia	Bamboo Ranch Club
Friday	November 9, 1962	Birmingham, Alabama	National Guard Armory
Saturday	November 10, 1962	Columbus, Georgia	(To Be Designated)
Sunday	November 11, 1962	Atlanta, Georgia	Magnolia Ballroom
Monday	November 12, 1962	Mobile, Alabama	Fort Whiting Aduitorium
Wednesday	November 14, 1962	Jackson, Mississippi	College Park Auditorium
Friday	November 16, 1962	Durham, North Carolina	City Armory
Saturday	November 17, 1962	Columbia, South Carolina	Township Auditorium
Tuesday	November 20, 1962	Greensville, South Carolina	Civic Auditorium
Wednesday	November 21, 1962	Tampa, Florida	Paladium
Thursday	November 22, 1962	Jacksonville, Florida	Coliseum
Friday	November 23, 1962	Macon, Georgia	Auditorium
Saturday	November 24, 1962	Daytona Beach, Florida	National Guard Armory
Sunday	November 25, 1962	Miami, Florida	Harlem Square
Saturday	December 1, 1962	Memphis, Tennessee	City Auditorium
December 7th thru 16th, 1962		New York, New York	Apollo Theatre

*****

(Itinerary Subject To Change)

WATCH FOR ANNOUNCEMENTS IN YOUR LOCAL AREAS - VIA POSTERS, NEWSPAPERS, RADIO AND T. V.

*****

MOTOR TOWN SPECIAL SHOW

featuring

Mary Wells   Miracles
Marv Johnson   Marvelettes
Contours   Marvin Gaye
Supremes   Vandellas
Singin' Sammy Ward   Bill Murry, M.C.
        Choker Campbell and his Show of Stars Band

The itinerary from the very first
Motor Town Revue
Courtesy R.ALLEN

10. Brenda Holloway

Brenda Holloway

When Motown opened their California headquarters in hopes of securing talent form the West Coast, one of the first discoveries was Brenda Holloway.

Brenda was a native Californian and would commute to and from Detroit for her recording sessions. While with Motown, Brenda had two very successful releases: "Every Little Bit Hurts" and "What Are You going To Do When I'm Gone". Released in May 1964, "Every Little Bit Hurts" became a hit for Holloway, reaching #13 on the Billboard Charts and helping to win the singer a concert spot on Dick Clark's "Caravan of Stars" tour. It was thanks to Brenda that The Supremes were taken on one of Dick Clark's tours. He wanted Brenda so badly for the tour that he took the then unknown Supremes along just to get Brenda. Holloway became a fixture on several 1960s television programs including *Shindig!* , and was later asked by The Beatles to open for them on their US tour in 1965. Holloway performed in the first rock stadium concert at for the Beatles as their opening act. Holloway was only one of three female acts who opencd for the Beatles; the other two were Mary Wells and Jackie DeShannon .   While Brenda was a fine performer, she proved to be very adept at songwriting. She also was one of the few female artists in Motown to write her own songs, and had a much grittier approach to songs than her contemporaries at the label. Between 1966 and early 1968, Holloway recorded a string of singles that were to be put on her second album, *Hurtin' & Cryin',* which was never officially released. Its first single was "Just Look What You've Done", which hit the Top 30 on the R & B charts. Its follow-up was

"You've Made Me So Very Happy ", was one of the few singles written by Holloway allowed to be released. The single peaked at number 39 on the pop chart and number 40 on the R&B chart. Holloway left Motown in 1968. A year later, Holloway received royalties for "You've Made Me So Very Happy" when Blood, Sweat and Tears took it to number 2 on the US pop chart and the Top 40 in the UK singles chart. One year later, Holloway retired from performing.

Brenda was a very religious girl, and she quickly tired of show business. She moved home to California and still resides there.

UPDATE: Holloway married a pastor and left the music industry to become a housewife. During this period, she occasionally sang with her sister Patrice. In 1980, Holloway briefly emerged from retirement to record a gospel album. After Holloway and her husband were divorced, she returned to performing secular music in 1988, recording for the UK label Motor City Records , which often released material of former Motown artists. In 1990 Holloway issued the album *All It Takes*. After the 1992 death of her friend Mary Wells, Holloway again emerged from retirement and resumed performing and recording. Her most recent album, *My Love is Your Love*, was released in 2003.

11. The Isley Brothers

The Isley Brothers

Ron, Rudolph, and O'Kelly Isley came to Motown by way of Atlantic Records in the mid-sixties. They had enjoyed some success with such hits as "Shout" and "Twist and Shout", which would later become a huge hit for The Beatles.

While their years with Motown didn't produce that many hit records, they did have two sizable hits with "I Guess I've Always Loved You" and "This Old Heart Of Mine". While they had modest success with other songs following its release, the group again struggled with a follow-up and in late 1968, were allowed to leave Motown. While at the crossroads of their career, the group toured the United Kingdom, where they had a following. Returning to the United States, they revamped T-Neck, a small label they had started some years before coming to Detroit.

A lot of problems the Isleys encountered at Motown were due to creative differences with Berry Gordy. Gordy wanted the Isleys to soften their style of music. They were strictly a rhythm and blues act, while Motown wanted their acts to appeal to everyone. In 1964, the group hired a young guitarist who had been in several rhythm and blues groups as a backing guitarist. His name was Jimi Hendrix, but was then going by his nickname at the time, Jimmy James. Hendrix, who was homeless when O'Kelly Isley saw him while at a store, was brought in to the Isleys' family home, and soon Hendrix was included in recordings the group was doing for T-Neck, two of which, "Testify " and

"Move Over and Let Me Dance", were released locally. By 1966 Hendrix had left the group, reportedly for being too flashy and taking away from the Isleys show, and he toured with Little Richard while The Isley Brothers the group signed with Motown Records after accepting a deal from Berry Gordy , who had promised to bring the group crossover success. That year, they had their first hit in four years with the pop-friendly "This Old Heart Of Mine" , which peaked at number eleven on the Hot 100.

While the Isleys were at Motown, they went to Berry Gordy with a song they wished to record titled, "It's Your Thing, Do What You Want to Do". Gordy refused and explained that it wasn't the type of song he wanted them recording. Eventually the Isleys left Motown and reformed their own record company, T-Neck Records, where they are today (1982). The group shelved the tune for later release and it went on to become the group's biggest hit when they released it as their first single on their own label.

UPDATE: *In 1991, Pullman Bonds made a deal with Isley Brothers founders Rudolph and Ronald Isley and the estate of O'Kelly Isley, Jr. to give the group unearned royalties from their extensive catalog. That same year, the surviving two brothers sued Michael Bolton, accusing the singer of copyright infringement for singing their 1964 song, "Love is a Wonderful Thing", which they wrote, without their permission. While Bolton insisted he didn't steal from the group, a judge awarded damages to Rudolph and Ronald after noting that while their songs, with the same titles, were different, elements of the songs were similar to each other. Bolton tried overturning the ruling on appeal in 2001, but was again defeated in court and forced to share writing credits of his hit with the brothers. This success revamped interest in the Isley Brothers and while Rudolph insisted on staying retired, Ronald, Ernie Isley and Marvin Isley reformed the group. The group's billing was also slightly changed to *The Isley Brothers* *featuring Ronald Isley* to reflect Ronald's desire to be seen as the group's dominant leader. Later that year, they released the album, *Tracks of Life.*

A year later, with one of their biggest admirers, Little Richard , the group was inducted into the Rock & Roll Hall of Fame. In 2001, the Isley Brothers scored their biggest hit in years when they released the R. Kelly-produced ballad, "Contagious", which peaked at number nineteen on the Billboard Hot 100 and number three on the R&B chart. Because of this, they had become the only group to chart in six decades. The song went platinum, selling over a million copies, while its parent album, *Eternal* , with its title track lyrics written by Ernie, sold over three million copies alone in the states. Two years later, their follow-up album, *Body Kiss* , became their first album to debut at number one on the Billboard 200 becoming their first number-one pop album since 1975's *The Heat Is On*, later going gold. On July 30, 2003, the group performed in front of its largest audience ever when they played in the afternoon during Molson Canadian Rocks for Toronto, a benefit to help raise the city's failing economy during the SARS crisis.

*Wikipedia

12. Chuck Jackson

If voice alone was the criteria for a recording artist to become a star, then Chuck Jackson should have been in the superstar category.

The management at Motown felt that Chuck had probably the finest male singing voice of any of their singers. They were unable, however, to parlay that voice into a hit record during Chuck's stay at Motown. He had some success at various other companies, with his biggest hit being "Any Day Now"; and in fact Chuck was one of the first artists to record material by Burt Bacharach and Hal David successfully . Chuck Jackson had all of the tools to become a big star. He was a dynamic entertainer on stage, with good looks that made him quite popular with the ladies. Chuck's biggest problem was the fact that he oversold every line of each song. An audience just isn't ready to sit and listen to a whole night of show stopping music.

Chuck had a big influence on Tom Jones' career. While Chuck was performing in the New York area, he had a constant fan standing in the wings watching every move--Tom Jones. Even today, Jones uses much of what he learned watching Chuck Jackson perform.

Eventually, Chuck left Motown and recorded for other companies. He still tours regularly and is very much into writing and producing. He's always willing to give young performers a helping hand, and they couldn't have a better teacher.

UPDATE: * In 1998 Jackson teamed with longtime friend Dionne Warwick to record "If I Let Myself Go", arranged as a duet by Wallert for Wave Entertainment. The recording received critical acclaim and charted at number 19 on the highly competitive Gavin Adult Contemporary Charts. Jackson followed with "What Goes Around, Comes Around", another Wallert production and composition, and reached number 13 on the Gavin Charts.

Several of Jackson's songs later became hits for other artists, including Ronnie Milsap whose 1982 cover version of "Any Day Now" reached #1 on the Country and Adult Contemporary charts, and Michael McDonald , who covered "I Keep Forgettin'" with great success. Jackson was close friends with political strategist Lee Atwater. He appears in the award-winning documentary "Boogie Man: The Lee Atwater Story."

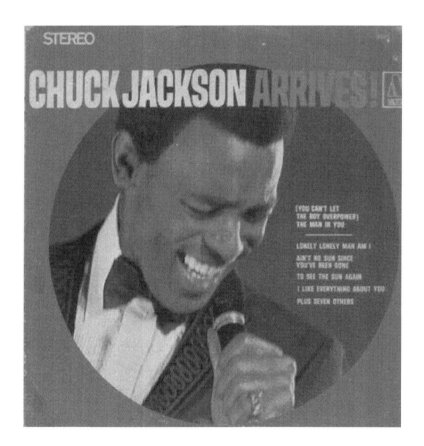

13. The Jackson 5

There have been many family acts in show business history, but few have made an impact like The Jackson 5 did in 1969.

Michael, Tito, Jermaine, Marlon and Jackie Jackson had turned professional several years earlier at the urging of their parents, Joe and Katherine Jackson. Joe Jackson had been a musician with The Falcons, a group who had a big hit in 1959 titled "You're So Fine". Jackson got his children interested in music as an alternative to the street gangs in their hometown of Gary, Indiana.

The Jacksons worked around the Indiana area at various clubs, parties, and local talent shows with good results. It's not all that unusual for young singing groups to be popular in a "cute" sort of way, but the Jacksons transcended that cute charm with some real talent. With Michael Jackson singing lead and his brothers backing him up, many people knew it was just a matter of time before the Jacksons would hit it big . Showing extraordinary talent at a very young age, Michael began demonstrating his dance moves and singing ability at the age of four. Michael's stunning rendition of "Climb Every Mountain" sung at his kindergarten talent show earned him a place in his brother's group. Prior to his eighth birthday, Michael was allowed to perform his song-and-dance routine at a talent contest held at Jackie's Roosevelt High School in Gary, helping his brothers win the competition

THE JACKSON FIVE & JOHNNY

This photo is probably the first publicity
photo taken of The Jacksons
Photo Courtesy EDWARD PATTEN

While working in Chicago on a show with Bobby Taylor and The Vancouvers, the youngsters so impressed the veteran Motown performers that they had the Vancouvers talking about them all the way home to Detroit. When Bobby got back to the Motown studios, he hurried into Berry Gordy's office to tell him about the young Jacksons. The reason I make such a point of how the Jacksons came to Motown's attention is because so much has been said about Diana Ross discovering the group. In fact, Bobby Taylor, not Diana Ross, brought the Jacksons to Motown's attention. Diana Ross was indeed instrumental in the Jacksons career as you will soon see but she didn't discover them as is widely reported.

In the late 1960's Richard Hatch, who was running for mayor of Gary, Indiana, asked Berry Gordy if he could supply some talent for a fundraiser he was having in Gary. Gordy sent down some of his artists, including Diana Ross, and saw this as a perfect opportunity to audition the Jacksons.

The Jacksons were added to the show and when the other Motown artists on the show saw the youngsters perform, they were flabbergasted at their poise and professionalism. Diana Ross was particularly impressed with the group, and it was at her urging that Berry Gordy signed the group. An audition was arranged in Detroit, and the Jacksons came to the Motor City. Joseph and The Jackson 5 stayed on the floor of Bobby Taylor's Detroit apartment the night of July 22, while Taylor and Motown executive Suzanne de Passe arranged for the Jackson 5 to audition for the label.

On July 23, the Jackson 5 had their Motown audition. Berry Gordy was not in attendance, but the audition was videotaped and sent to him in Las Angeles. Gordy's initial reluctance to sign the group disappeared when he finally saw the boys perform. Gordy decided to sign the Jackson 5 to Motown, and hosted a party at his Detroit mansion on November 25, 1968, to introduce them to the Motown staff and stars.

The Jackson 5, couldn't have come along at a better time for Motown. Many of their top groups such as Martha and The Vandellas, The Four Tops and The Spinners, had left the company for greener pastures. It had been eight years since Motown had recorded their first hit song and their listening audience had changed dramatically in that time. The Jackson 5 proved to be a much needed shot in the arm for Motown. They were marketed primarily to the pre-and early teen audience that was in their age group.

In 1970, The Jackson Five first released "I Want You Back" which went to number one on the charts and sold over three million copies. "I Want You Back ", was written and produced by four Motown songwriters and producers — Berry Gordy, Alphonzo Mizell, Deke Richards, and Freddie Peren— who were collectively billed as "The Corporation ". They followed up with six straight million sellers that all went to number one on the charts. Such hits as "A.B.C.", "I'll Be There", and "Never Can Say Goodbye" made The Jackson Five the hottest property Motown had. To be more specific, they were the top selling group of 1970, and with their popularity among their fans, they became superstars. "Jacksonmania" swept the nation, and within a year of their debut The Jackson 5 were among the biggest names in popular music. The group essentially replaced The Supremes as Motown's main marketing focus, and capitalizing upon the youth-oriented appeal of the Jackson brothers, Motown licensed dozens of Jackson 5-related juvenile products, including the now famous J5 Heart logo which appears on Johnny Jackson's drum kit and many of The Jackson 5's album covers, stickers , sew able patches, posters, and coloring books.

In spite of their youth, The Jackson 5 were master showmen in the true Motown sense. Their costuming and choreography were right out of the Motown handbook, and wherever they performed, the concerts were sellouts. In 1971, with their popularity at its peak, The Jackson 5 starred in their own television special titled, "Going Back to Indiana", which featured the group in concert as well as footage of their hometown area. The show was so well received, it led to a Jackson 5 cartoon series as well as a complete line of souvenirs.

It became obvious by 1972 that Michael Jackson had that certain appeal which set him apart from the rest of the group. In 1971, Motown began a spin-off solo career for Michael, whose first single, "Got To Be There " became a Top 5 hit. Michael also sang the title track for the 1972 movie *Ben*. His other successful solo singles included

"Rockin Robin " and "I Wanna Be Where You Are" (both 1972). Jackie also recorded a solo album in 1973, but his releases failed to chart. Despite fan rumors that all three Jacksons might leave the group as they released solo work, the solo careers of Michael, Jermaine, and Jackie co-existed alongside that of the group as a whole, allowing Motown to expand the success and sales of Jackson 5-related releases.

 It was decided that brother Jermaine should be given a shot at a solo project. His release of "Daddy's Home" did well for him and proved once again that one of the Jacksons could stand out from the group and stand tall. While on the subject of Jermaine, I should note that he is the husband of Hazel Gordy, Berry's daughter. When the two were married in 1973, Gordy threw one of the biggest weddings ever seen in the Detroit area. It had been rumored that the cost of the wedding was nearly $200,000.

In the 70's the Jacksons saw their popularity challenged by a group of clean-cut youngsters who grew up before the American public on the Andy Williams show. They were known as The Osmonds, and before long, their popularity would rival that of the Jacksons. Unfortunately, the rivalry would be split along racial lines. Whenever either group would play, the house would be sold out with white audiences for the Osmonds and black audiences for The Jacksons. Another aspect of this competition was the rapid decline of the Jacksons record sales. Obviously the white teens had indeed been buying the groups records, but then The Osmonds arrived o the scene, their allegiance shifted dramatically.

In 1974, The Jackson 5 had one last big smash with Motown when they hit the top of the charts with "Dancin' Machine." Feeling that The Jackson 5 could be more of a success without Motown, which was by this time declining in success and popularity, Joseph began shopping for a new record deal for his sons.

TITO   JACKIE
MICHAEL   RANDY   MARLON

A 1981 Photo of The Jacksons

In 1976, The Jacksons left Motown, leaving brother Jermaine behind. He remained loyal to Motown and quickly established himself as a mainstay in the Motown lineup in California. The rest of the family moved on to Epic Records where, besides Michael's solo projects, they had very little success selling records. The Jackson 5 went through a name change as well. It was decided that Motown had exclusive rights to the name Jackson 5, so the group was renamed The Jacksons. Even though their record sales have dipped, they still remain a huge concert attraction, mostly due to Michael. He has enjoyed great success in his solo career, and even won a starring role opposite Diana Ross as the Scarecrow in "The Wiz".

UPDATE: In 1979, The Jacksons received a star on the Hollywood Walk of Fame . In 1978, Michael starred alongside Diana Ross in the Motown/Universal Pictures motion picture *The Wiz*, based upon L. Frank Baum's *The Wonderful Wizard Of Oz*. Quincy Jones was the producer of the film's songs, and he and Michael began work on Michael's first Epic solo album, *Off The Wall* , the next year. *Off the Wall*, released in 1979, sold 20 million copies worldwide and featured four Top 10 hit singles and two number one singles, causing some speculation about whether Michael would leave The Jacksons, even though Michael told several reporters that the rumors were unfounded.

The group's success was outperformed, however, by Michael's 1982 LP *Thriller*. *Thriller* went on to become the most successful album ever in the United States, and to date stands as the world's best-selling album of all time. The Motown 25 television special, broadcast on NBC on May 16, 1983, featured a reunion performance between Jermaine and the other brothers. Outside of one 1979 appearance on the TV show Midnight Special, this was the original Jackson 5's first performance in nearly seven years. The *Motown 25* Jackson 5 reunion was overshadowed, however, by Michael's performance of "Billie Jean " on the same program, which introduced his trademark black sequin jacket, single decorated glove and "Moonwalk" dance.

The subsequent Victory Tour of North America in the summer and fall of 1984 proved to be one of the biggest concert tours of the 1980s. Aside from a few scattered TV and concert appearances in the 1970s, the Victory Tour period was the only time all six brothers performed together as full members of the band.

Michael left the band to continue his solo career after the tour. Marlon left around the same time to pursue a business career outside music. The other brothers took on solo projects. Most of them would appear with Michael on the U.S.A. For Africa single "We Are The World" in 1985.

The last Jacksons album was *2300 Jackson Street* in 1989. Every Jackson sibling except for LaToya appeared on the title track, a #9 R&B hit single. The rest of the album featured Jermaine, Jackie, Tito and Randy only. In September 2001, The Jacksons reunited to perform at a concert special at Madison Square Garden to celebrate 30 years of Michael Jackson's career as a solo artist. The concerts were filmed and the footage was shown in the special, *30th Anniversary Celebration*, which aired on CBS in November 2001 as a two-hour television special.

In June 2009, following the death of brother Michael, the remaining performing Jacksons reunited in a studio to record background vocals for a previously unreleased song, "This Is It ", which had originally been a demo. The radio-only single was released in October of that same year. The song did not chart on the *Billboard* Hot 100. "This Is It" returned The Jacksons to the chart for the first time since 1970 when, billed as the Jackson 5, the group marked its sole previous entry, "I'll Be There", which went on to peak on the chart at number twenty-four. The surviving members of the Jacksons were in talks for planning a reunion concert tour (which was to be served as a tribute to Michael) for 2010, and discussed working on their first new studio album in over 20 years. However, neither plan has been put into action. In September 2010, Jermaine Jackson held his own "tribute" concert to Michael in Las Vegas . While his brothers and sister Janet attended, none of them joined their brother onstage. As of March 2011, the future of the Jacksons remains uncertain as Jackie Jackson released a solo single to iTunes and both Jermaine and Tito Jackson are planning to release new solo studio albums. Marlon Jackson retired from the music business in 1989.

14. Marv Johnson

Although he never had a hit record with Motown, Marv Johnson was very much a part of the Motown scene.

Back in 1959, Marv was the second recording artist Berry Gordy signed the first being The Miracles. Gordy had already decided to form his first record label ,Tamla , and Johnson's recording of "Come to Me" became the label's first single release in May 1959. Gordy didn't have a record company at that time, so all of the material he was recording on various artists was being leased out to other companies. This was the case with the Marv Johnson tune titled "You've Got What It Takes", a top ten hit for Marv in 1959 on United Artists records. That song proved to be the biggest hit Marv Johnson had in his career. He toured with the various Motown shows, but he never had a hit with Motown.

Johnson was extremely popular in Europe, where he toured extensively. He, as much as any artist, took the "Motown Sound" to Europe where he gave it thorough exposure. When he retired from performing, he worked as a record distributor for Motown.

Today (1982) Johnson lives in Detroit and is no longer in the music business.

UPDATE: After issuing his final Motown singles in 1968, Johnson remained with Motown working on sales and promotion throughout the 1970s. Johnson continued singing into the 1990s, releasing a solo album on the London based Motor City Records label. Johnson died of a stroke on 16 May 1993, in Columbia ,South Carolina, at the age of 54. He is interred at Woodlawn Cemetery in Detroit .

15. Gladys Knight & The Pips

Early Motown publicity photo

Gladys Knight & The Pips came to Motown Record Company with one thing mind: stardom. They not only achieved their goal, but surpassed it in their seven years with Motown.

As Gladys tells it, "We were appearing since we were small children and we had been preparing ourselves for the moment when we would have our big chance at stardom. Motown gave us a chance to get our foot in a lot of doors we had been unable to open ourselves. "

It wasn't an easy decision for the group to go to Motown. They knew they would be starting at the bottom of the Motown list. Even so, the bottom of Motown was a very prestigious point for many artists. There were nagging questions that haunted Gladys, who was very much against the move. She felt the Motown system was far too structured and controlled for her liking. She also felt that Motown wouldn't sincerely promote another female besides Diana Ross, who was unquestionably the crown jewel of Motown.

Despite her suspicions, Gladys went along with her cousins, William and Edward, and her brother Bubba, who were all very much in favor of the move. They saw Motown as the springboard to television and nightclubs which were uncharted territories for many blacks at the time. Motown acts were showing up in such prestigious locations as Las Vegas and New York night spots, as well as on the top rated Ed Sullivan Show.

The Motown Sound was capturing a lot of white ears that Gladys Knight & The Pips had been missing at other record companies. The move to Motown was designed to help them capture those white listeners.

Edward Patton, one of the Pips, tells the story. "Working Las Vegas and the Ed Sullivan Show were dreams we worked for since we began in the business. We became personal favorites of Ed's and he invited us back several times personally. The exposure those shows gave us benefited us to this day."

From L to R
William Guest
Gladys Knight
Edward Patrten
Bubba Knight

During their seven years with Motown, many things came to pass that both Gladys & The Pips had predicted The stardom and exposure they had sought came to them, putting them in the superstar category. With such hits as "My Imagination", "Friendship Train", "Neither One Of Us" and their biggest of all, "Heard It Through The Grapevine" (which at the time was the biggest song the Motown Company had) the group had begun to capture that listening audience they had always been searching for. The record sold 2.5 million copies, and at the time was Motown's best-selling single ever. Producer Norman Whitfield recorded four versions of the song with various artists for potential single release; Knight and the Pips' version was the only one that Berry Gordy did not veto. Edward Patton also liked the family atmosphere at the West Grand Boulevard studios. "I like belonging to something, and the people at Motown were like one big family when the studios were on the Boulevard. It was a pleasure to get up and go to work. Many people would come down even if they weren't scheduled that day and just hang out."

William Quest, another of The Pips, tells of the main reason they came to Motown. "Cholly Atkins and Maurice King were the backbone of Motown's Artist Development Department when we got to Motown, but our relationship goes back to our early days in Atlanta. Maurice taught us voice and Cholly taught us choreography, so it was a real treat for us to be teamed up again." Gladys and The Pips were regulars at Artist Development, and when others would cancel their time, The Pips would slide in. This was in addition to their regularly scheduled practice sessions.

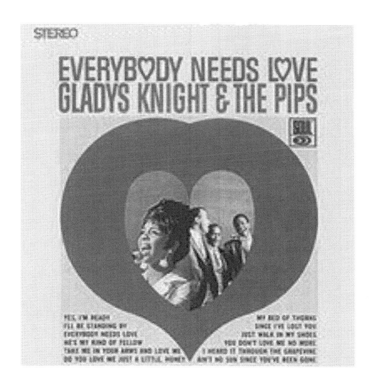

A 1970 photo of Gladys Knight and the
Pips

As Gladys told me, "When we signed with Motown, Berry Gordy told us that he was tired of hearing how good Gladys Knight & The Pips were. The reason we were so good was because we never stopped trying to improve our act." Bubba Knight added an interesting point to what Gladys said. "We had to pay for many things that Motown furnished for their acts, such as Artist Development. We took advantage of everything they had to offer which could improve our act."

Many of the things offered at Motown were not to the liking of the group. As I mentioned earlier, one of the drawbacks Gladys perceived was that the Motown system was far too structured for them. She also felt because of the number of groups they had at Motown, The Pips might not get the type of attention they had hoped for. You must remember that Gladys Knight & The Pips had been headliners since 1957, so they weren't as inexperienced as many of the artists on the Motown roster. "When we came with Motown, we signed a seven year contract and at that point, Motown took total control of our career," Edward Patton told me. "We were given a Motown manager, a Motown lawyer, and the only person we were able to bring with us was our accountant who is now our personal manager. I didn't think it was very fair to have one company in total control of your career, especially since we were all paid by the same boss." William Quest put it a bit stronger: "It was obviously a conflict of interests. I suppose we could have gotten out of our contract, but we were enjoying great success, so we didn't rock the boat."

Gladys and Bubba Knight took a somewhat psychological approach to the whole situation. While at Motown, Knight & The Pips recorded for Soul Records, a label Motown used for acts that recorded material with more of an R&B flavor than a pop flavor. On the A&E Network television program *Biography* , Knight stated that she and the Pips were regarded as a second-string act, and that "The Supremes ,The Temptations , and Marvin Gaye were given all the hits, while we took the leftovers." In Knight's autobiography *Between Each Line of Pain and Glory: My Life Story*, she stated that Diana Ross had the group removed from being The Supremes' opening act on a 1968 tour for, according to Knight, being *too* good.

Motown would have open auditions each week, and these served as a reminder that a singer could always be replaced. Ever since Mary Wells had left the company in the mid-sixties, her career had faltered. So Motown always had ammunition to frighten the other performers.

Although Motown was enjoying great monetary success, there was evidence that the company was growing out of its small family atmosphere. Many incompetent people were being hired because they were old friends of Berry's or they were relatives. This was about the time that the company relocated to the Donovan building on Woodward in Detroit. Many people felt that it was at this time that Motown lost the personal atmosphere which had been the cornerstone of its success.

The Pips related several instances of incompetence. "Once we were sent to the wrong town to perform by one of our new managers. On another occasion, Berry Gordy's nephew, who had never been involved in show business, came to watch us rehearse. As we were rehearsing our act he started giving us pointers on what we were doing wrong in our choreography. Can you imagine that? We had been doing our act for twenty years, and this kid is going to improve our act for us in five minutes."

These sort of interferences were becoming harder and harder to deal with when the group's contract was coming up for renewal. It was an almost forgone conclusion that you would renew your contract with Motown. As negotiations opened on a new contract, it was quite obvious that money was going to be a big stumbling block. Edward and William explained, " We were offered $40, 000 to renew with Motown and we felt it was way below our worth. We had shopped around and we knew what our worth really was. We countered with an offer of one million dollars. We were encouraged to take such an offer if some record company would be foolish enough to make the offer. They didn't know we had such an offer from a competitor, who was quite eager to have our services. So when we were given a way out, we took it."

At this point, Motown's incompetence shows up more than ever. The group recorded "Midnight Train To Georgia" as their first release on their new label and upon its success, Berry Gordy called the producer who had been working with Gladys and The Pips to congratulate him on a job well done. It was only at this point that Berry Gordy was made aware that Gladys Knight & The Pips were no longer with Motown. The most notable hit of their career, "Midnight Train To Georgia ", won the Grammy for Best R&B Group of 1973. The song eventually received the Grammy Hall Of Fame Award, which was established by the Recording Academy's National Trustees to honor recordings of lasting qualitative or historical significance.

Aboard the USS Ranger Nov 1981

Gladys Knight & the Pips have gone on to have monumental success since their Motown days. Much of that success can be attributed to Motown itself. In retrospect the feeling exists that they remain grateful to Motown for the doors they opened for the group. In turn, I am sure Motown is equally grateful to Gladys Knight & The Pips. During their seven years with the company they helped put Motown on the top of the music industry and keep it there. As Gladys and The Pips put it, "We wouldn't trade our years with Motown for anything." I'm sure Motown feels the same way.

UPDATE: Knight and the Pips continued to have R&B hits until the late 1980s, very briefly adding a fourth member, Chris Morante, in 1988. From 1978 to 1980, Knight and The Pips were forced to record separately due to legal problems with Buddah. Knight released two solo albums and The Pips released two albums of their own. In 1977, the Pips (minus Gladys) appeared on comedian Richard Pryor's TV special that aired on NBC . They sang their normal backup verses for the songs "Heard it Through the Grapevine" and "Midnight Train to Georgia;" during the parts where Gladys would sing, the camera panned on a lone-standing microphone.

After an international tour, Knight and The Pips recorded the LP *Visions* (1983), which resulted in a #1 R&B hit with "Save The Overtime (For Me) " and was certified gold. In 1987, Knight and the Pips released their final album, *All Our Love*, on MCA Records which was also certified gold. The album's single "Love Overboard" became a #1 R&B hit which won the 1988 Grammy for Best R&B Performance by a Duo or Group with Vocals. In 1988 the band also won a Soul Train Music Award For Career Achievement . Gladys Knight & the Pips embarked on their final tour in 1988 and disbanded upon its conclusion, as Gladys Knight decided she wanted to pursue a solo career. The Pips retired, while Gladys Knight began scoring hits of her own with singles such as "Men"

(1991) and "I Don't Want to Know" (1994).The group was inducted into the Rock & Roll Hall of Fame in 1996, the Vocal Group Hall of Fame in 2001 and received a Lifetime Achievement Award from the Rhythm & Blues Foundation in 1998. Ms. Knight continues to tour and record occasionally, and leads the Saints Unified Vocal choir. Edward Patten of The Pips died in February 2005, of complications from his long bout with diabetes.

Gladys Knight & The Pips are ranked as the ninth most successful act in *The Billboard Top 40 Book of R&B and Hip-Hop Hits* (2005). They were also ranked #91 on VH1's *Top 100 Artists of Rock n' Roll.* In June 2006, Gladys Knight & the Pips were inducted into the Apollo Theater 's Hall Of Fame in New York City.

In 2007, The Pips appeared in a commercial for the auto insurance company Geico . As Edward Patten had died two years prior, one of Gladys Knight's current backing singers, Neil Taffe , accompanied the remaining Pips.

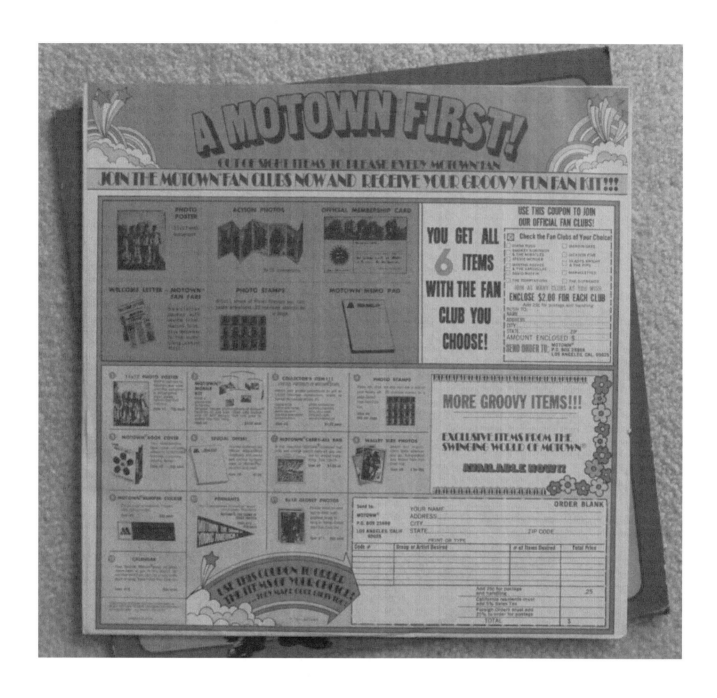

On the paper sleeve of the records was information on how to join the Motown Fan Club and get great Motown stuff. Each artist had their own club.

16. Shorty Long

Shorty Long was one of the finest comedians and emcees Motown had. He was highly regarded in and around the Detroit area, working in a host of local clubs. He was a terrific organ player and had several releases which gained him some attention, most notably "Devil With The Blue Dress On", "Here Comes Da Judge", and his most famous, "Function At The Junction". Long came to Motown in 1963 from the Tri-Phi/Harvey label, owned by Berry Gordy's sister, Gwen, and her husband, Harvey Fuqua. His first release, "Devil With The Blue Dress On" (1964), written with William "Mickey" Stevenson, was the first recording issued on Motown's Soul label, a subsidiary designed for more blues-based artists such as Long. Marvin Gaye, in David Ritz's biography *Divided Soul: The Life & Times of Marvin Gaye*, described Shorty Long as "this beautiful cat who had two hits, and then got ignored by Motown." Gaye claimed he "fought for guys like Shorty" while at Motown, since no one ever pushed for these artists.

Shorty was used mostly as a part of the Motown package tours sent out on the road with Choker Campbell and The All Stars as the band. He would serve as the show's emcee after he had done his act.

Shorty had been working in clubs around the Detroit and Windsor area when his untimely death occurred while boating on the Detroit River.

Update:* On June 29, 1969, Long and a friend drowned when their boat capsized on the Detroit River in Michigan. Stevie Wonder played the harmonica at his burial, and placed it on his casket afterwards. Writer Roger Green's epitaph stated: "So there endeth the career of a man who sang what he wanted to sing - everything from the blues to romantic ballads, from wild and crazy numbers to a utopian vision of Heaven on Earth. Short in stature but big in talent, he entertained and amazed us, and finally he inspired us."

Motown issued Long's final album, *The Prime of Shorty Long*, shortly after his death.

Source: Wikipedia

17. The Marvelettes

THE MARVELETTES

The odds against The Marvelettes making it in the music business were astronomical, but due to their spirit and a few helping hands along the way, they not only made it, they delivered Motown Record's first number one song, "Please Mr. Postman".

The Marvelettes' story begins at a talent show at Inkster High School. Inkster is a suburb of Detroit and all The Marvelettes grew up there. Five high school friends got together and formed a singing group to compete in the talent show. The three finalists were to be given auditions with a newly formed record company in Detroit called Motown Records.

The Marvelettes finished fourth in that talent show, but because an administrator at the school felt they had worked so hard they should not miss out on the audition with Motown; she implored the Motown talent scout John O'Denn, who was at the show, to give the girls a tryout. Gladys Horton, an original member of the group, recalls that first meeting at the Motown offices. "We were all high school students when we went to Motown for our audition and we were all very impressionable. After all, no one was over 16 years old. The group was made up of me, Katherine Anderson, Juanita Cowart, Georgeanna Gordon, and Georgia Dobbins, who wrote, "Please, Mr. Postman". After we were auditioned by Robert Bateman and John O'Denn, it was decided we should work on some original material and come back at a later date. That's when Georgia wrote "Postman". When we came back in April of 1961, Berry Gordy liked what he heard of "Please, Mr. Postman", so after some fine tuning by some of the Motown writers, we recorded it. It was released in August of 1961 and by December, we had the number one song in the country." To say the least, Motown officials were quite surprised to have their first number one song recorded by a group of high school students.

The Marvelettes strut their stuff at the
Motortown Revue 1963

Because of family obligations, Georgia Dobbins left the group. Juanita Cowart decided show business wasn't her cup of tea, and she dropped out, as well. Wanda Rogers joined the group at this time, and it was decided to leave the group at four members.

Katherine Anderson remembers what it was like to be a high school student with the number one record in the nation. "We were all quite naive when we signed with Motown, and in the beginning we were only able to work on weekends because of our schooling. But after a while, we hired a tutor so we would be able to work more often and not fall behind in our studies. By the time we graduated, we had two other big hits, "Playboy", and "Beachwood 45789". We were in constant demand for concerts and at the time it was all very exciting for us."

Shortly after graduation from high school, Georgeanna Gordon was forced to leave the group but remained with Motown as a secretary, and it was decided to leave the group with three members. More hits followed, such as "Too Many Fish In The Sea", "Don't Mess With Bill", and "The Hunter Gets Captured By The Game". The Marvelettes became prototypes for many other singing groups of the day such as the Crystals, Chiffons, and The Shangri- Las. If you recall, it became quite popular to use three girls in singing groups at the time.

Gladys Horton remembers how everyone pulled for each other in those early days at Motown: "There was a lot of love in that building on West Grand Boulevard. Everyone pulled for each other to put out a hit and when they did, we were all happy for them. We were having a great time and money was the last thing on our minds at the time. We weren't paid very much, but we were young and really didn't care. "

Gladys might not have cared about money at the time, but looking back on it now, she is more perturbed by what she feels was a lack of recognition by Motown where The Marvelettes were concerned. When "Please, Mr. Postman" became a big hit, not many people knew about Motown records. "I feel that because the postman was a universal symbol and recognized world-wide, it was the reason that the tune became a big hit all over the world. Because it was a world-wide hit, it carried the Motown name as well. I don't think we ever got the credit we deserved, and I know Berry Gordy is well aware that it was four high school girls who gave him his first number one record," Gladys says.

Katherine Anderson isn't quite as adamant as Gladys, but she shares the same feelings about the reason "Postman" was such a huge success. "Everyone knows the postman all over the world and everybody had been waiting for a letter from a loved one at one time in their life. That's why I think the song was so popular, particularly among servicemen."

The Marvelettes' success lasted only a few years, as Motown produced more and more successful groups. They had periodic hits, but for the most part, their most successful years were behind them as the late 60's approached. It's very hard to imagine someone's career being over by their mid-twenties, but that's pretty much the way it happened with The Marvelettes. They began to have a lot of internal problems, and Gladys Horton left the group after the birth of her first child. A replacement was found and the group remained together, hoping to find the magic they once had known, but with release of "My Body Must Be A Magician", it marked the last hit record The Marvelettes would produce. Now married, Katherine Anderson Shafner sums up her feelings about her years at Motown with The Marvelettes: "If someone would have told me what I would experience, both good and bad, I probably wouldn't have believed them. We were just kids when we went to work with Motown, and I probably would have done things differently. It was still quite a thrill for me." Today (1982), Katherine is happily married and still lives in Inkster with her husband and family. I was unable to get in touch with Wanda Rogers, but I was told she resides in Detroit and is no longer involved in the music business.

Gladys Horton, who contributed the most to this chapter, has reorganized The Marvelettes and is currently on the comeback trail(1982). The group had been working various clubs in the Detroit area and had a new album ready for release. She summed up her Motown Memories in this fashion: "Our age worked against us when we went with Motown. And I think we were very naïve about financial matters of the record business, but it was still a great experience being with the top record company in America and it was fabulous being stars right in our own hometown."

In retrospect I feel that Motown and The Marvelettes can thank each other for the success they both enjoyed in those early days of Motown.

Update: * In 2006, Horton appeared with Dazee Luv, Jaki-G & Denise Stubbs of Joe Harris' Undisputed Truth on PBSs *My Music Salute to Early Motown.*

An in-depth history of the group can be found in Marc Taylor's book, *The Original Marvelettes: Motown's Mystery Girl Group* and the *Goldmine* article on the group from its June 8, 1984 issue.

In 2007, the Marvelettes were inducted into the Michigan Rock and Roll Legends Hall of Fame.

In 2009, as part of Motown's 50th Anniversary celebrations, a new limited-edition triple-CD set on the group entitled *The Marvelettes: Forever – The Complete Motown Albums Vol. 1* was released. This featured the group's first six albums, some of which had never been released on CD. *Vol. 2* is scheduled for release in 2011.

- **Wanda Young Rogers**

Rogers currently lives in the Detroit suburb of Westland, Michigan. She made a brief return to performing in the early 1990s as a solo artist, re-recording some of the Marvelettes' hits, such as "Don't Mess With Bill". Her last public appearance was in early 2006 when she attended a play hosted by Katherine Anderson Schaffner.

- **Katherine Anderson**

Katherine Elaine Anderson Schaffner retired from singing when the group disbanded in 1972 (the year Motown moved to Los Angeles). She has become very involved in helping troubled teenagers in the Detroit area. She appeared in 2006 to attend a play in her home town of Inkster, Michigan, where she still lives. Her last appearance was at the Motown 50th Anniversary, held at the Roostertail in Detroit on November 21, 2009. Katherine (Kat to her friends) is the mother of two adult children, Keisha and Kalaine Schaffner. She is also the grandmother of one grandson, Toure Schaffner. Of all the original Marvelettes, Katherine is the most active today. She was one of the writers of the Gladys Knight & The Pips hit, "I Don't Want To Do Wrong."

- **Gladys Horton**

Gladys Catherine Horton semi-retired from the business to take care of her handicapped son; however, she still performed on occasion as "Gladys Horton of the Marvelettes". She had lived in southern California since the early 1970s. She died at age 66 on January 26, 2011, at a nursing home in Sherman Oaks, California following several strokes.

- **Georgeanna Tillman**

On August 12, 1963, Georgeanna Marie Tillman married Billy Gordon of The Contours ; she left the group about two years later. On January 6, 1980, she died from complications of lupus and sickle-cell anemia , at age 36. She is interred at the Metropolitan Memorial Park in Belleville, Michigan

- **Juanita Cowart**

Juanita Cowart Motley officially left the Marvelettes back in the late winter/early spring of 1962 (though she would occasionally record with the group until early 1963). Shortly after, she bought a candy store on Michigan Avenue in her neighborhood of Inkster, Michigan with $1,500.00 she had saved as a Marvelettes. Her last appearance in public was in 2006 when she attended a play in her home town of Inkster, Michigan, where she still lives.

- **Ann Bogan**

After the Marvelettes disbanded in 1972, Anne Bogan went on to lead an RCA trio known as Love, Peace & Happiness , which was part of the group New Birth . Ann settled into a secure nine-to-five job in Cleveland. She is alive and well in Cleveland, Ohio, and sings with a gospel group.

* Wikipedia

SMOKEY ROBINSON

Writer, producer, singer, executive

18. The Miracles

Of all of the music sung by the groups of Motown, the most beautiful of all was sung by The Miracles.

Originally the group was known as The Matadors, and they sang around various talent shows in the Detroit area; shortly after Bobby Rogers joined the group, they changed their name to The Miracles. While auditioning at a club in Detroit, they chanced to meet Berry Gordy, Jr. who was visiting the club with Jackie Wilson.

The Miracles didn't get the job at that club, but the day proved to be one of the luckiest days of their career. Having failed the audition, Berry Gordy asked the group if they needed someone to produce their records for them. At the time Gordy, besides writing some material for Jackie Wilson, was an independent record producer who made master recordings for local artists. As you can imagine, the young teenagers jumped at the chance to make a record. Bobby Rogers remembers that those first recordings weren't the most successful records The Miracles ever recorded. "We did a couple of early tunes that Berry sold, but they never went anywhere. When he got back to Detroit he was quite discouraged and that's when he decided to start his own label. That was in 1959 and that's pretty much how Motown started. "

In 1959, when Motown started, The Miracles were one of the very first acts signed. At the time, the group was made up of Smokey and Claudette Robinson, Pete Moore, Ron White, and Bobby Rogers. The company was short on everything but talent in those days, so everyone served in whatever capacity they were needed. Smokey Robinson was a fine writer of music, so it fell to his shoulders to write and produce music for The Miracles, as well as other groups. The Miracles themselves would provide instrumentation and sing back-up on the records.

One of the first artists Smokey worked with was a young girl who would become the first female star at Motown. Her name was Mary Wells, and Smokey Robinson recalls the material he produced for her quite fondly: "I worked with Mary from 1959 until 1963 and I found creating music for other people to be a great thrill. It proved to be a whole new aspect of the business for me. Before Mary, I had concentrated solely on songs for The Miracles and it was one of by biggest thrills when "My Guy" hit number one for Mary in 1964."

As far as thrills go, The Miracles and Berry Gordy shared a great thrill back in 1961, when their recording of "Shop Around" sold a million copies and gave the fledgling company a big lift. Its sales kept the company going while they were struggling to get on their feet. In the wake of this success, the Miracles became the first-ever Motown act to perform on Dick Clark's American Bandstand on December 27, 1960. Shortly after "Shop Around", Motown started putting out more and more quality material, but getting that material on the air was quite a different story.

Bobby Rogers recalls some of the tricks they used to get the radio stations to play their songs. "When we first started to record on Motown, our music was considered Race Music and white radio stations were a bit reluctant to play our songs. If they did play it, they would play just a portion of it to lead into the news or a commercial. We finally decided to put a shorter time on the record than it actually lasted. If it lasted three minutes, we would print two minutes and ten seconds on the label. That way they began to play the recordings just to fill up a short period of time, but by the time they were aware of what was happening, the record was over." Someone must have been listening, because by 1963, they had two other hit records out titled "You've Got A Hold On Me", and "Mickey's Monkey".

The Miracles were in constant demand for personal appearances due to their enormous popularity, but the hectic schedule took its toll on Claudette Robinson. During those rigorous touring years , she suffered two miscarriages and it was decided that she would leave the group and take life a bit easier.

The sound of The Miracles stayed the same and more hits followed, including ,"Ooo Baby, Baby" and The Tracks Of My Tears". It was at this time that Smokey began producing material for another group Motown was quite high on, The Temptations. He produced several hit songs for The Temptations, but his crowning glory was a tune called "My Girl", which gave The Temptations their first million selling song and put them on their way to super stardom.

Smokey and The Miracles after Claudette left the group

Motown Records were reaching marvelous new heights and The Miracles' career was enjoying the same type of success. One of the main reasons the company enjoyed this success was due in part to the many talented Detroiters being brought in to the company by the current groups under contract. Two such talents The Miracles uncovered were three young ladies they auditioned called The Primettes who would later become The Supremes and a young blind child, who lived down the street from Ronny White. The young boy would sit in front of his house playing a harmonica all day long. Ronny brought him to Berry Gordy, who immediately signed him. Today you know him as Stevie Wonder. Despite all the success The Miracles were having, the group decided to retire back in the 60's. This is when Smokey Robinson became a Vice President with Motown so he could learn the business end of the recording industry. The other Miracles took various front office jobs with the company.

Bobby Rogers explains why the group would make such a decision at the height of their career. "Being on the road can be quite a grind and we felt we needed a rest. We had all done quite well financially, so we thought it would be a good time to enter the business end of Motown and see how that worked. Smokey really enjoyed the inner workings of the business very much, but Pete, Ronny and I tired quickly of our office jobs. After about a year we grew restless for the stage, and we finally got Smokey to admit he'd like to perform again. When we were all in agreement, we went back into the studio, cut some material, and began to perform live again. Most of our fans didn't know we had retired because Motown continued to release records we had already recorded. Aside from no personal appearances, it was though we were doing business as usual."

Once back doing live performances, Smokey Robinson and The Miracles, as they were now being called, produced just as before with such hits as "I Second That Emotion", and the Tracks Of My Tears". Their audiences were glad to have them back as well, and their concerts were sellouts from coast to coast. Berry Gordy was equally glad to have them doing what they did best--performing.

As The Miracles entered the 70's, the rumored move of Motown to the West Coast became a reality. The group was split on the move; Smokey wanted to make the move, but The Miracles wanted to stay in their hometown. Smokey also wanted to get back into the creative side of his work. Over the years, Smokey had created some of the most beautiful music Motown had recorded. He explains what sort of ideas helped him create that music: "My best ideas had to do with love and sadness. They are real emotions which everyone can identify with. My upbeat material was more for fun, but the real audience reaction came from the sad love songs."

With these objectives in mind, it was decided among the whole group, and with Berry Gordy as well, that due to Smokey's desire to enter the creative aspects of Motown on a full time basis, he would leave The Miracles. A date was set for Smokey's departure and The Miracles set out to replace Smokey Robinson. The Miracles took a long time auditioning a replacement for Smokey, but finally one was found. His name was Bill Griffin and he came from Baltimore, Maryland. He had a sound which seemed to fit perfectly with The Miracles.

I say "Seemed to" because Bill had a very difficult time adjusting to being Smokey's replacement. People would always ask why Smokey wasn't with the group and that bothered Bill.

It wasn't until The Miracles struck gold with the million selling "Love Machine" that they proved to all the skeptics that they could still make it without the presence of Smokey Robinson. There was no animosity involved with Smokey leaving the group; it was strictly a personal decision which everyone accepted. I feel I should make that quite clear.

When Smokey Robinson left The Miracles

Bill Griffin(Back Row)Joined the group

I'm sure, though, everyone was relieved to receive a gold record without Smokey's voice on it.

Problems arose between The Miracles and Motown Records when it came time to renew their contract. The company was in the middle of a contract squabble with Stevie Wonder at the time, and they requested The Miracles wait six months to begin contract talks. Bobby Rodgers relates what transpired in those six months: "We felt we were being snubbed by the Motown brass, and to be perfectly honest, we were upset by the treatment. When CBS heard we hadn't signed with Motown, they came to us with a tremendous offer we couldn't pass up. They were in the process of signing a lot of black groups at this time, so they wasted very little time signing us up. " It wasn't long after they signed with CBS Records that the group split up for good.

After a lengthy European tour, Pete Moore decided he no longer wanted to be on the road, and Bill Griffin wanted a solo career. Unable to reach any sort of compromise, The Miracles, who had started twenty years earlier, disbanded.

In the following years, Smokey Robinson's solo career reached fantastic new heights as he released several number one hits with Motown. He continued to serve the company in a management capacity as well as a performer. He and his wife Claudette live in California with their children (1982).

Pete Moore retired as an active performer and he too lives in California. (1982)

Bobby Rogers and Ron White live comfortably in Detroit where they have begun to reassemble the New Miracles. (1982)

It is safe to assume that whenever people mention Motown Records, they will mention Smokey Robinson and The Miracles. That is a marvelous legacy to leave behind.

UPDATE:

Past Members:	Members:
Smokey Robinson	Bobby Rogers
Ronald White (deceased)	Claudette Rogers Robinson
Pete Moore	Dave Finley
Marv Tarplin	Tee Turner
Billy Griffin	Mark Scott
Sidney Justin	
Donald Griffin	
Carl Cotton (deceased)	

Alphonse Franklin

James Grice

Emerson "Sonny" Rogers

Clarence Dawson

In 2004, *Rolling Stone* magazine ranked Smokey Robinson & the Miracles #32 on their list of "The Immortals: 100 Greatest Artists of All Time." They are also ranked in the Top 100 Artists Of All Time on Billboard Magazine's and Vh-1's 1998 lists.

Today, original member Pete Moore is owner and CEO of his own Las Vegas-based entertainment firm, WBMM Enterprises. He and his wife Tina are parents to twin daughters, Monette and Monique.

Bobby Rogers tours nationally and internationally with the current Miracles group. Divorced from his first wife, Marvelettes member Wanda Young and now re-married for many years to current wife Joan, he has 4 grown children: Bobbae, Gina, Robert III and Kimberly.

Ronnie White became an affluent real estate developer*. He died at the age of 57, and is survived by his wife, Gloria, a son, Ron II, and a daughter, Pamela. His first wife, Earlyn and eldest daughter Michelle, preceded him in death.

Claudette Robinson is the First Lady of Motown, an active board member of the National Rhythm and Blues Foundation, HAL (Heroes & Legends) Awards, and she continues to perform at selected concerts with the Miracles. She is also writing her memoirs for publication. She and Smokey are now divorced and have two grown children, Berry and Tamla.

Marv Tarplin and his former wife, Sylvia, have a daughter, Talese. The couple divorced, and Sylvia died in 2004. Marv retired from touring in 2008.

Smokey Robinson owns a food corporation, *Smokey Robinson Foods,* and continues to tour and record as a solo artist. His current wife is Frances Glandney, and he has another son, Trey Robinson.

The original Miracles Bobby Rogers, Pete Moore, Claudette Robinson and Smokey Robinson, re-united in Detroit in 2007 to celebrate the group's 50th anniversary, and performed in a tribute to Motown founder Berry Gordy.

In 2006, Woodbridge Estates, an exclusive residential development in The City of Detroit, named their community park "Miracles Park" and one of its streets "Miracles Boulevard" in recognition of the legendary Motown group's importance to the city, and as a tribute to their many accomplishments in the music industry. To date, The Miracles have sold over 40,000,000 records worldwide, and have won numerous Gold and Platinum Records and other music industry awards. In 2006, the original Miracles were inducted into the Michigan Rock and Roll Legends Hall of Fame. In 2008, the group's recording of "The Tracks Of My Tears" was voted a Legendary Michigan Song.

Despite the inductions of many of their Motown labelmates, as of 2011, the Miracles, Motown's first group and the artists most responsible for establishing the label's early success, still have not been inducted into the Rock and Roll Hall Of Fame.

Motown founder and first president Berry Gordy Jr. said: "Without The Miracles, Motown would not be the Motown it is today".

19. The Monitors

The Monitors

The Monitors were one of the hardest working and most reliable groups that worked at Motown. They initially started out as the Majestics but because another group was using that name, it was decided by Motown executive Taylor Cox that they should change their name to The Monitors. The group, which consisted of lead singer Richard Street, Sandra Fagin, John "Maurice" Fagin, and Warren Harris, had only one minor hit, a cover of the Valadiers' "Greetings".

The group was a regular on the Motor Town Revues that toured the country and worked as an opening act for many of the top Motown acts. After a particularly good performance at the Detroit stop of the Motortown Revue, Berry Gordy called a meeting of his top production people and told them to work on material for The Monitors. The group recorded several songs that got some air play: "Say You", "Since I Lost You Girl", and "Greeting", but they weren't the big hits Motown was looking for. They were switched to Motown's SOUL label with "Step by Step (Hand in Hand)" in the summer of 1968, but this was to be their final single with Motown. However, they also released an album, "Greetings! We're The Monitors", in 1968.

The Monitors eventually disbanded, but one of the members, Richard Street, took Paul Williams' spot with The Temptations when Paul became unable to perform any longer. Richard is still a member of The Temptations today, but The Monitors remain a fond Motown memory.

Update: British producer Ian Levine recorded a new version of The Monitors in the late 1980s, with lead singer Darrell Littlejohn (a nephew of Smokey Robinson), Warren Harris, Maurice Fagin, Herschel Hunter, and Leah Harris, but without Richard Street. The group released a new album, *Grazing in the Grass*, on Levine's Motorcity label.

Motown drummer Uriel Jones
Photo Courtesy EARL VAN DYKE

20. The Motown Musicians

The Funk Brothers

James Jamerson, Dan Turner, Earl Van
Dyke
Photo Courtesy EARL VAN DYKE

The "Motown Sound" is one of those intangibles that elude definition. Many people have tried to define it, and just as many have failed.

One thing for certain is that the "Motown Sound" was brought to life by a group of musicians who worked in a basement studio, which came to be known as "The Snakepit". These men were the musicians of Motown and they were affectionately known as "The Funk Brothers". This group was made up at its core by Joe Hunter, Benny Benjamin, James Jamison, Robert White, Eddie Willis, and Earl Van Dyke.

James Jamerson-A Funk Brother guitarist
Photo Courtesy EARL VAN DYKE

Other musicians were added at various times, but more or less, these men were the heart and soul of "The Motown Sound". So adept were these musicians that they came to know exactly what sound each producer was looking for. The producers for the most part had a healthy and great respect for the musicians, and allowed each man his individuality on the records.

Thomas (Beans)Bowles, who served as a
musician with Motown,
before he joined their management team
Photo CourtesyT. BOWLES

Earl Van Dyke relates a humorous story of how a new producer learned to respect "The Snakepit" and its craftsmen: "Berry Gordy's brother, George, came downstairs one day to produce some material. He took the attitude that we didn't understand what he wanted, and he started giving us orders. We had been recording Motown music for quite some time, and this was George's first attempt at producing a record, so we decided to have some fun with him. Instead of putting anything special into the session, we played exactly what was put in front of us. George couldn't understand why the sound he wanted wasn't coming out on the recording. After several hours, he called us all together and asked what the problem was. We told him to go into the control booth and leave us alone and we would record the material. In the next hour, we recorded four songs exactly the way he wanted. It was our way of showing him that we knew our business and could deliver almost anything a producer wanted, if he showed us some respect."

Robert White -Guitarist with Motown's
rhtym section

Something should be pointed out about the ability of these gifted musicians and artists. Some of the producers in the early days would come down to the recording studio with just a chord sheet and no other music. They would all collaborate with each other and before long, a song was born. As Thomas "Beans" Bowles recalls, Berry Gordy himself had very little else when he did his first recordings. "I got a call one night from Berry, to meet him at his apartment. He wanted to record a song on Marv Johnson and he needed some help with the music. All we had to work with was Berry's ideas and some chords. Eventually we went down to United Sound and recorded the tune. It was a very crude beginning, but that's how the first Motown material was recorded."

Although most of the musicians worked in total obscurity, one person who gave them his respect was Berry Gordy. Gordy knew first hand how much they could do with so little to work with. When he was financially able, he saw to it that any and all problems they had were taken care of. He also saw to it that any instrument that was needed was provided.

A case in point involves a Wurlitzer organ that Berry wanted Earl Van Dyke to play. Earl wasn't keen on the idea of learning the instrument and he made it quite clear to his boss. Gordy asked Earl if he wouldn't mind going to the music store and taking a look at the organ. Berry wanted to purchase the organ for the studio and he valued Earl's opinion. When Van Dyke reported back to Gordy's office, he told Berry that the organ was quite nice and would make a fine addition to the studio if Berry decided to purchase it. The next morning when all of the musicians assembled in the studio, that same Wurlitzer organ was sitting there. Earl Van Dyke became a master of that organ-- the same one he declined to play initially.

Earl Van Dyke

Thomas "Beans" Bowles, who had helped Berry Gordy with his first recording, joined the Motown Corporation as a musician. It wasn't long though, before Bowles moved into the management end of Motown. However, before he did this, his saxophone could be heard on most of the early recordings of Mary Wells, The Marvelettes, The Miracles, and Marvin Gaye.

One song in particular that "Beans" played on holds a special memory for him. "I played flute on the first album we recorded on Stevie Wonder. We took him over to the Regal Theater in Chicago to perform and record a live album. I served as a sort of road manager for this tour and I'll never forget watching that twelve year old kid steal the show. We had to have Stevie off the stage by ten o'clock, so he would perform early in the show. His last song was "Fingertips" and when he was through his mentor, Clarence Paul, would usher him off the stage. Even at 12, Stevie was quite a showman and he ran back to the microphone and started singing, "Everybody say Yea!" and the crowd picked up the chant. He started into "Fingertips" again, catching the orchestra off guard. If you listen closely, you can hear the conductor asking Stevie, "What key? What key?" The crowd went crazy over Stevie, and the resulting album and single both hit the number one spot on the charts."

Eddie Willis was another of The Funk Brothers. He was a guitarist of great range and one of the very first musicians who worked with Motown. Eddie recalls the first record he worked on for Berry Gordy. "I grew up with Marv Johnson, so we knew each other very well. When Marv was to record some tunes at United Sound for Berry Gordy, he asked if I could play on the session with him. This is when Berry was still an independent producer, so I guess I was in on the ground floor of Motown."

Eddie Willis -Guitar and Sitar

The term "Funk Brothers" has been used several times in this chapter, and I suppose I should explain how the term came about. A lot of producers who would come downstairs to the recording studio would ask the musicians to play a tune "funky". James Jamison picked up on the term and decided to call the group of musicians "The Funk Brothers". The name stuck, and whenever any of the Motown musicians speak of each other, they refer to themselves as "The Funk Brothers".

One notable thing about Motown's studio musicians is that they rarely worked outside of the recording studio. Only on the rare occasion when one of the more prominent Motown performers demanded to have The Funk Brothers back them up in a live performance would Berry Gordy let them out of the studio. Gordy even had a special kitchen set up.

When the musicians were going full out in the studio sessions, Berry Gordy noticed that it paid to keep them in the studio recording, Occasionally, when some of the musicians would go out to lunch, they would lose their continuity or worse yet, "get lost" and not return at all. With 10 or 15 groups recording all of the time, it was imperative that the musicians keep working. He finally decided to hire a cook for his kitchen, whom the musicians affectionately called "Tomaine Annie" Annie would fix lunches for the employees, and they would all go outside and have a picnic. Berry Gordy, in his infinite wisdom, not only kept his musicians in the studio area, he cultivated a family type atmosphere among his employees.

The Motown Record Corporation, in time, was growing out of its West Grand Boulevard location, so Berry Gordy sought a new location which he found on Woodward Avenue in Detroit. Everyone was moved into the new location except the musicians. Earl Van Dyke recalls how the musicians felt about that. "We were all hurt that we were left behind. It seemed that we weren't given any consideration. But we found out, in the long run, we were far better off staying right where we were. On the occasions when we would to down to the new building, we found there was a great deal of confusion in the new offices. "

Eddie Willis had a different look at what happened during the move over to Woodward Avenue: "Things seemed to change a lot when the company moved to the new building. The family atmosphere that we all enjoyed in the early days was now gone. One thing that never changed for the musicians that stayed in the old building was our sound. I feel part of the reason we always sounded the same was because we stayed in our familiar surroundings. "

Pistol Allen, who was a studio
drummer with Motown
Photo Courtesy R. ALLEN

The musicians of Motown all took a great deal of pride in their work, as you would expect. There wasn't a great deal of recognition but Richard "Pistol" Allen recalls that, every now and then, one of the groups would request a studio musician to go out on tour with them. "I can recall getting various requests from artists requesting that I accompany them on a particular tour. They wanted to make sure their live performance sounded like their recordings. Many other studio musicians were put into service as road musicians for the same reason. "

Allen, who was a drummer, provided the beat for many songs that required his specialty; the Shuffle beat".
That beat can be heard on such hits as "Come And Get These Memories" , "Uptight", "Heat Wave", and "Baby Love". Allen, like most of the Motown musicians, had developed their own style, and in their unique ways, they blended those styles into what came to be known as "The Motown Sound"". Allen, like the others I spoke to, had long since left the Motown scene. He sums up his feelings in a way that could speak for all those men who worked so hard in the basement of the Motown Studio. "Whenever we hear a record we worked on at Motown, we can pick out the various styles. That is our tribute, and it will live on forever, especially in the hearts of the musicians who created that special style."

The San Remo Golden Strings

As the productions and songs from Motown grew more complex, the producers began to expand from blues into orchestral arrangements. This made it necessary to obtain the talents of string players and horns with some need of a concert master to blend these artists with The Funk Brothers. From the Detroit Symphony and the Windsor Symphony came players who worked on various Motown productions. They sat in with The Funk Brothers and made the magic of Smokey Robinson, Holland, Dozier, and Holland, and Ashford and Simpson swell to grander realms than Motown had attempted before. The Funk Brothers, although not classically trained, made these arrangements beautiful, and, without question Motown-sounding recordings.

Some of the players of the San Remo Strings are believed to be:

Violins

ZINOVI BISTRITZKY
BEATRIZ BUDINSZKY
LILLIAN DOWNS
VIRGINIA HALFMANN
RICHARD MARGITZA
FELIX RESNICK
ALVIN SCORE
LINDA SNEDDEN SMITH
JAMES WARING

Violas
NATHAN GORDON
DAVID IRELAND
EDOUARD KESNER
ANNE MISCHAKOFF
MEYER SHAPIRO

Cellos

ITALO BABINI
EDWARD KORKIGIAN
THADDEUS MARKIEWICZ
MARCY SCHWEICKHARDT

Harps
CAROLE CROSBY
PAT TERRY

Percussion
ROBERT PANGBORN

Concert master, first violinist and contractor, Gordon Staples.

Funk Brother Members:

Joe Hunter* (keyboards, 1959-'64)
Robert White* (guitar, 1959-'72)
Eddie Willis* (guitar, 1959-'72)
Joe Messina* (guitar, 1959-'72)
James Jamerson* (bass, 1959-'72)
Marvin Gaye (drums,1959–'62)
Benny Benjamin* (drums, 1959-'69)
Richard "Pistol" Allen* (drums, 1959-'72)
Jack Ashford* (percussion, 1959-'72)
Eddie "Bongo" Brown* (percussion, 1959-'72)
Johnny Griffith* (keyboards, 1963-'72)
Uriel Jones* (drums, 1963-'72)
Earl Van Dyke* (keyboards, 1964-'72)
Bob Babbitt* (bass, 1967-'72)
Dennis Coffey (guitar, 1967-'73)
* official member

UDATE:

The Funk Brothers were dismissed in 1972, when Berry Gordy moved the entire Motown label to Los Angeles—an arrangement some of the musicians discovered only from a notice on the studio door. A few members, including James Jamerson, followed to the West Coast, but found the environment uncomfortable. For many of the L.A. recordings, members of the Wrecking Crew--the prominent group of session musicians including drummer Earl Palmer, bassist Carol Kaye , guitar master Tommy Tedesco, and keyboard genius Larry Knechtel--joined the team at Motown.

In March 2006, some remaining Funk Brothers were invited to perform on Philadelphia writer/producer/singer Phil Hurtt's unique and interesting recording session at Studio A/Dearborn Heights/Detroit where they contributed their performances to "The Soulful Tale of Two Cities" project. The double album sleeve notes read 'Motown's legendary Funk Brothers and members of Philadelphia's world renown MFSB take you "back in the day" with an album filled with classic Philly and Motown hits". Bob Babbitt, Joe Hunter , Uriel Jones, and Eddie Willis performed alongside other notable Detroit session musicians like Ray Monette, Robert Jones, Spider Webb, and Treaty Womack. The musicians played on the Philly hits giving their unique Detroit interpretations of the songs under the leadership of Phil Hurtt, Bobby Eli, Clay McMurray and Lamont Dozier. Many other ex-Motown and Detroit artists performed vocals on the session including The Velvelettes, Carolyn Crawford, Lamont Dozier, Bobby Taylor, Kim Weston, Freda Payne, and George Clinton.

In 2008Uriel Jones , Ray Monette, Dennis Coffey, Robert Jones and Bob Babbitt accompanied other notable Detroit session musicians including Larry Fratangelo, Dennis Sheridan, Edward Gooch, John Trudell, George Benson, Mark Burger, David Jennings, Spider Webb, and Rob Pipho on the Carl Dixon Bandtraxs project which featured a Dennis Coffey/Carl Dixon production of four brand new songs. In addition vocal performances from Spyder Turner, Pree and Gayle Butts provided lead and backing for the session. The session was also arranged by ex-Motown arranger David J. Van De Pitte. The session was held at Studio A, Dearborn Heights, Detroit and was the dream of a 19 year old Dixon, back in 1974, to pay homage to musicians, particularly The Funk Brothers, producers and those who influenced him with their music. It took Dixon almost 33 years to find the musicians and, with luck, he met some of them on the web site soulfuldetroit.com. It was via this web site that he and Dennis Coffee hooked up and then eventually collaborated to make the session work.

In 2010, surviving members of the Funk Brothers accompanied Phil Collins on his Motown covers album *Going Back.*

This chapter has been dedicated to those men who worked in relative obscurity for many years. You, who created a sound that became world famous, take a bow.

21. The Originals

THE ORIGINALS
Soul Recording Artists

The Originals, like many of the groups at Motown, were very talented but just couldn't get their career off the ground. It wasn't for lack of effort for The Originals were always to be found in the Motown rehearsal halls working on their act.

During their career with Motown, the group had two releases which did moderately well on the charts, "Bells", and "Baby I'm For Real". The Originals were made up of Hank Walter, Freddie Gordon, Henry Gaines and former Spinner, C. P. Spencer.

Motown worked hard trying to get The Originals off the ground. They served as opening acts for most of the major Motown attractions, so they weren't lacking for exposure. It's hard to understand why some groups captured the magic of Motown, while others, no less talented, worked hard with no results.

The Originals served Motown in many background capacities during their time there. You may have heard them singing in the background many times on your favorite Motown hit.

Members:

Hank Dixon
Dillon Gorman
Terrie Dixon
Defrantz Forrest

Past Members:

Freddie Gorman (deceased)
Walter Gaines
Ty Hunter (deceased)
C.P. Spencer (deceased)
Joe Stubbs (deceased)

Update: Joe Stubbs, brother of Four Tops' lead, Levi Stubbs, died on February 5, 1998. He had been with the group for about six months in the mid 1960s, and was also a former member of The Falcons, The Contours and 100 Proof. C.P. Spencer died on October 20, 2004 and Freddie Gorman followed on June 13, 2006.

Following the death of Freddie Gorman in 2006, founding member Hank Dixon and Hank's daughter Terrie Dixon reformed the Originals as a live touring act, with Freddie's son Dillon Gorman and Defrantz Forrest, son of Gene Chandler ("The Duke of Earl").

22. Rare Earth

Rare Earth was unique in Motown history for several reasons, one of which was the fact that Berry Gordy recorded the group on Rare Earth Records. They ushered in the Psychedelic sound to Motown, and they were far and away the most successful white group Motown had.

The group formed in 1960 as The Sunliners and changed their name to Rare Earth in 1968. After recording an unsuccessful album *Dream/Answers* on the Verve label in 1968, they were signed to Motown in 1969.

When the group was brought to Motown's attention, Berry Gordy saw the chance to capitalize on the group's popularity among teenagers who were very much into the new Psychedelic music craze. The group's first two single releases were remakes of old Temptations songs, "Losing You" and "Gettin' Ready". As Rare Earth lead singer Pete Horlbeck recalls it was quite natural for the group to record those tunes. "We had been doing "Losing You" and "Gettin' Ready" in our act all along, so when Motown executives decided we should release them as singles, it seemed perfectly logical."

The group followed those hits with two other releases which did even better, "Big Brother" and "I Just Want to Celebrate". These successful recordings proved that the faith Barnet Ales showed in the group was well placed. Ales was a vice president at Motown at the time and was very instrumental in Rare Earth's success.

When Motown moved to the West Coast, Rare Earth was part of the move, but it wasn't long before the group, suffering from internal problems, broke up in the mid seventies. Motown was a bit reluctant to see one of their top groups sitting on the sidelines, so in 1978 they regrouped at the Motown studios in California to record two albums. Unfortunately, they did very little in sales and the group disbanded once again.

In 1980, after a couple of years of inactivity, the original Rare Earth got back together and signed with RCA Records. They are currently (1982) touring and recording, hoping to find that success they knew at Motown.

Members:

Gil Bridges
Ray Monette
Randy "Bird" Burghdoff
Mike Bruner
Floyd Stokes Jr.

Past Members:

Peter Rivera (Hoorelbeke)
Rod Richards
John Persh
Ivan Greilich
Eddie Guzman
Mike Urso
Ray Monette
Kenny James
Reggie McBride
Dan Ferguson
Jerry LaCroix
Paul Warren
Gabriel Katona
Ken Johnston

UPDATE: * Other than Mike Bruner's succeeding Rick Warner in January 1998 and Ivan Greilich's filling in for Ray Monette for five years (beginning in 2004), the lineup has been stable overall during the last decade or so.

Rare Earth continues to perform at corporate events and on the oldies circuit. Bits from their recordings have been used as samples on recordings as diverse as: Beck's "Derelict", UNKLE, and DJ Shadow's "GDMFSOB, Peanut Butter Wolf's "Tale of Five Cities", Scarface's "Faith", NWA's "Real Niggaz Don't Die" and Eric B and Rankim's

"What's Going On". In 2005, Rare Earth was inducted into the Michigan Rock and Roll Legends Hall of Fame.

Their hit "I Just Want to Celebrate" has been used in major national advertising campaigns by Ford Motor Company and AT&T . On October 27 & 28, 2007, heavy metal band Metallica performed "I Just Want to Celebrate" during their acoustic performances at Neil Young's Bridge School Benefit show.

* Wikipedia

23. Jimmy Ruffin

Jimmy Ruffin came to Motown Records as a result of Berry Gordy's purchase of Golden World Records, which was the "other" top record company in Detroit.

Jimmy Ruffin had what one Motown executive told me was an identity problem, due to his brother David, who was the charismatic lead singer of The Temptations. Jimmy Ruffin had a tremendous voice that produced several top ten hits while he was recording for Motown.

Such tunes as "Gonna Give Her All The Love I've Got", "I've Passed This Way Before" and his biggest hit, "What Becomes Of The Broken Hearted" made Jimmy a huge success in Europe, where he was in constant demand. The intended follow-up, "East Side-West Side, was released only in Australia, due to an argument by Berry Gordy . Unfortunate, he was never able to transfer that popularity to American audiences.

He was used primarily as an opening act for various other Motown acts and was a mainstay of the ever popular Motor Town Revues. Jimmy Ruffin eventually left Motown and worked quite a bit in Europe and when last heard of, had recorded an album for R.S.O Records (1982).

UPDATE : * In the 1980s Ruffin moved to live in Britain, where he continued to perform successfully. In December 1984 he collaborated with Paul Weller of The Style Council for his benefit single "Soul Deep." This went under the name of The Council Collective and Jimmy appeared with Paul on Radio 1 in Britain to say he is involved because his father worked down the mines and "he understands the suffering." In 1986 he collaborated with the British group Heaven 17 , singing "A Foolish Thing To Do" and "My Sensitivity" on a EP record. He also recorded duets with both Maxine Nightingale and Brenda Holloway . Later, Ruffin hosted a radio show in the UK for a time, and became an anti-drug advocate following the death of his brother David in 1991. Ruffin was portrayed by Lamman Rucker in the 1998 *Temptations miniseries.*

Living in England, he continues to tour and perform.

Since January 2011, Jimmy Ruffin has been working on writing and recording songs for his new album which he plans to release on his 74th birthday,(May 7, 2013).

*Wikipedia

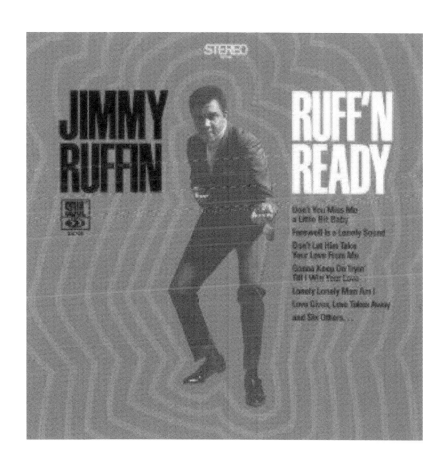

24. The Spinners

Henry Fambrough   Billy Henderson   John Edwards   Pervis Jackson   Bobbie Smith

THE SPINNERS

Back in 1955, five high school friends got together and formed a singing group known as The Domingos. Billy Henderson, Bobby Smith, Pervis Jackson, Henry Fambrough and C.P. Spencer were the five young Ferndale High students who would go on to become The Spinners. Like most groups of the era, if they were to make a name for themselves, they would have to compete in various amateur shows around the Detroit area. Bobby Smith related what it was like in those early days as a member of The Domingos. "We were very popular around the Ferndale area where we lived, but we knew we had to compete in some of the Detroit shows if we were going to get any real recognition. So we started competing against a lot of groups we would end up working with at Motown, such as The Temptations, and The Miracles. I remember one show we won at the Gold Coast Theater. We beat out Smokey and The Miracles. They were very popular, even back then, so we felt it was a real feather in our cap to win."

Shortly after that win, it was decided that the group would change their name to The Spinners. They worked at clubs around the Detroit and Toledo area until they met two sisters, Anna and Gwen Gordy, who, with Harvey Fuqua were starting up Anna-Tri Phi Records in Detroit. Harvey Fuqua worked with the group, polishing their style. He himself was a part of a famous group known as Harvey and The Moonglows, prior to his involvement with Anna-Tri- Phi Records.

Eventually, The Spinners released a recording which did quite well titled "That's What Girls Are Made For." Not long after the release, Tri-Phi Records merged with Motown Records, which was owned by the Gordy sisters' brother, Berry. That's how The Spinners became a part of the Motown scene.

It was not for lack of dedication or talent that The Spinners weren't as big a success with Motown as they should have been. There were a large number of similar groups such as The Temptations, The Miracles, and The Contours who were cranking out one hit record after the other at the time. There was another problem the group had--they couldn't put back to back hits together, which would have given they the selling power Motown was looking for in all their artists. They did record four sizable hits, which did well: "Sweet Things", "Truly Yours", "I'll Always Love You", and their biggest hit, "It's A Shame", which was written and produced by Stevie Wonder. In between hit records The Spinners were quite willing to do almost any odd job Motown had for them, and worked at jobs around the Motown offices. They worked as chauffeurs, delivery men, and janitors to stay on the Motown payroll. They reasoned that Motown was a very prestigious company at the time, and eventually they would get their break.

Pervis Jackson recalls that if it wasn't for Diana Ross and The Supremes, they wouldn't have been performing much at all. "Diana, Mary and Florence took a liking to us, and asked if we could work with them as their opening act when they performed. Because they were on the road so much, we received a great deal of exposure from the tours. It was a great thrill working with The Supremes, and we'll always owe them a great debt for the interest they showed in us."

Working with Motown had a lot of benefits, one of which was their Artist Development Department. The Spinners took full advantage of that department when they weren't performing. They were so diligent in their practices that they became one of the best choreographed groups Motown had. Henry Fambrough shares his insights on those days: "Because the more popular groups were on the road so much, they weren't using their practice time. Cholly Atkins and Maurice King, who were in charge of Artist Development, would ask us if we wanted to use the extra time. We would rush to get there before The Pips, who also used extra time in the Artist Development to hone their act. We always accepted and I'm sure it was to our benefit in the long run."

During their seven years with Motown, The Spinners remained intact for the most part, except for their fifth member. During that period they used C.P. Spencer, Chico Edwards, George Dixon, G. C. Cameron and Philippe Wynne as their lead singer. Such changes were very common among the male groups at Motown. Despite the personnel changes, one thing that remained the same was the group's unshakeable belief in themselves. Billy Henson reflects on the optimism the group shared: "Starting back when we were known as The Domingos, we always felt that if we stuck together, we'd make it. We believed in ourselves and our sound. We knew it was just a matter of time before everything would click for us. "

In 1971 when their contract with Motown ran out, the Spinners sought greener pastures. Although they were grateful to Motown, they felt they were being lost in the shuffle with all the male groups working there. Pervis Jackson echoes the group's sentiments, as he recalls the departure from Motown: "We weren't real pleased with the situation at Motown, so we were looking for a record company that didn't have so many male groups recording for them. We signed on with Atlantic Records and met a producer named Thom Bell who wanted to produce some things for us. We have enjoyed great success with Atlantic, and much of our success is due to the experiences we had at Motown."

To say The Spinners have enjoyed success at Atlantic Records would be quite an understatement. They have gone on to record numerous gold records, headline at the finest night spots in the world, and guest star on many major television shows. The group has never forgotten how tough a climb they had to the top, either. Several years ago, The Spinners Foundation was started to aid college students who need financial assistance to complete their studies. So far (1982), they have aided a music major at the University of Michigan, an accountant at Temple University, and a medical student at U.C.L.A. Several years ago, a lasting tribute to The Spinners was placed along Hollywood Boulevard, as The Spinners had a star placed on the famed Hollywood Walk of Fame-- true recognition for a group who never lost sight of where they were headed or where they had been.

UPDATE : * After their chart career ended, The Spinners continued touring for decades. Even though their last hits were almost 25 years ago, the bright lights of their 1972–1976 run of the charts continues to provide for the current members. They are big draws on the oldies and nostalgia concert circuits and continue to play the music that made them famous.

A voice from their past, G.C. Cameron, would rejoin the group as lead vocalist from 2000 to 2002 (replacing Jonathan Edwards, who left due to a stroke that left him wheelchair-bound), but he left them in 2003 to join The Temptations . Frank Washington, formerly of The Futures and The Delfonics, joined for a few years, before being replaced by Charlton Washington (no relation).

In 2004, original member Billy Henderson was dismissed from the group after suing the group's corporation and business manager to obtain financial records. He was replaced by Harold "Spike" Bonhart. Henderson died due to complications from diabetes on February 2, 2007 at the age of 67. Early member C.P. Spencer had already died from a heart attack on October 20, 2004.

The group lost another member from their starting days when Pervis Jackson , who was still touring as a member of the group, died of cancer on August 18, 2008. The group continued for a short time as a quartet before Jessie Robert Peck (born in Queens, New York, December 17, 1968) was recruited as the group's new bass vocalist in February 2009. In the Summer of 2009, Harold "Spike" Bonhart left the Spinners, and was replaced by vocalist Marvin Taylor. The group is actively touring with two of its surviving original members (Fambrough and Smith), Charlton Washington, Jessie Peck, and Marvin Taylor.*

* Wikipedia

Spinners first charted record

25. Edwin Starr

The name Edwin Starr is linked closely with Motown Records. The fact is, however, Edwin enjoyed his biggest success at Ric Tic Records with such hits as "Agent OO Soul". He also recorded for Golden World Records and when Motown purchased Golden World, Edwin became part of the Motown stable.

He became a very popular attraction at Motown, particularly with the female audiences due to his showmanship and good looks. While Edwin was with Motown he had only two big hits, "25 Miles to Go", and the anti-war message, "War".

Due to his popularity Edwin became a bit of a problem for executives at Motown. It seemed his ego was larger than his record sales, and Motown wasn't noted for catering to very many of their performers. So when Edwin decided to move on, Motown wasn't exactly heartbroken. Berry Gordy was starting to get into the movie business and he really wasn't concerned with keeping any performers other than his superstar acts. They also felt Edwin has seen better days as a recording star.

Edwin eventually migrated to California, where he has recorded with various labels trying to recapture the success he knew in Detroit.

UPDATE: * In 1973 Starr moved to England. In 1985, Starr released "It Ain't Fair". Despite garnering the attention of many in the soul and dance clubs, the song was not really a hit, certainly not the hit he was looking for.

In 1989, Starr also joined Ivan Levine's Motorcity Records , releasing six singles and the album *Where Is the Sound*, as well as co-writing several songs for other artists on the label. Starr resurfaced briefly in 2000 to team up with the UK band Utah Saints to record a new version of "Funky Music Sho Nuff Turns Me On". He appeared again in 2002 to record a song with Jools Holland , singing "Snowflake Boogie" on Holland's CD *More Friends* and to record another track with Utah Saints, a so-far-unreleased version of his number one hit "War" — his last-ever recording.

Starr remained a hero on England's Northern Soul circuit and continued living in England for the remainder of his life.

On Wednesday, April 2, 2003, at the age of 61, Starr suffered a heart attack and died while taking a bath at his home in Bramcote near Nottingham . He left a wife, Annette Mary Hatcher, a son André Hatcher, and two grandchildren Alonté Renfroe and Maryah Hatcher.

* Wikipedia

26. Barrett Strong

Barrett Strong in very early motown photo

Barrett Strong holds the distinction of being the first male star Motown ever produced. He recorded a tune which Berry Gordy and Janie Bradford-Hobbs wrote called "Money". This was the very first Motown hit record.

Barrett Strong was a friend of Berry Gordy. He joined Motown in its very earliest stages and stayed on to see the company gain its lofty status as the biggest record company in the world. Because there were very few people on the Motown payroll in those early days, Strong played piano, wrote, and sang on many of the company's early releases. Eventually he went into the production end of the business on a full time basis. Many fans aren't aware of it, but Barrett Strong had a hand in producing such hits as "I Heard It Through The Grapevine", "Psychedelic Shack", "Cloud Nine" and "I Wish It Would Rain".

You can see that Barrett Strong, who joined Motown at the beginning, was contributing factor to its success over the years.

He recently left the company (1982) to seek other business opportunities, but left his mark on the company he helped create and get off the ground.

UPDATE:* Strong left Motown when the label moved to Los Angeles in 1972, and he signed with Epic. After one failed single, Strong moved to Capitol where he had the LP *Stronghold* released in 1975 and later *Live & Love* in 1976. Though it wasn't a hit, his song "Man Up in the Sky" was a '70s soul landmark.

Strong continued into the '80s, recording "Rock It Easy" for an independent label and writing and arranging "You Can Depend on Me" which was included on The Dells' *The Second Time* LP in 1988.

* L A Times

THE SUPREMES

27. The Supremes

The Supremes circa 1965
Photo CourtesyR.ASHFORD-HOLMES

"From Little Acorns Does The Giant Oak Tree Grow."

If ever a group personified this saying it had to be The Supremes. Their backgrounds are what great stories are made of. Poor girls from a Detroit ghetto, they became the most popular female singing group of all time.

Such is the story of The Supremes. They started out like many of the Motown groups, singing on porch steps, street corners and school talent shows. Mary Wilson and Florence Ballard first met at a Junior High School talent show in Detroit. They both did quite well in the show and the girls decided that if the opportunity ever arose, they would like to form a singing group. A pact was made that if either girl was approached to join a singing group, the group would have to take them both.

Not long after that pact was made, Florence Ballard was contacted by two young men in the neighborhood who were singing in their own group called The Primes. They were interested in forming a sister group and wondered if Florence would be interested in joining. They had already lined up two other girls, but Florence convinced them to audition her friend, Mary Wilson.

I would like to stop at this point and give a little background information on The Primes and the two young men, Paul Williams and Eddie Kendricks. They grew up in the same neighborhood as Florence and Mary, and their group, The Primes, would one day become The Temptations.

At the impromptu audition were two other girls recruited by Paul and Eddie--Betty Travis and Diane Ross. (In time her name would be changed to Diana.) Florence and Mary were somewhat familiar with Diane, for she, too, lived in the same neighborhood. Betty Travis was a bit older than the other girls and in time that would become the reason she would leave the group. The audition proved successful for all of the girls and in the blink of an eye, The Primettes were born. A rather simple start for a group that would rewrite music history!

The Primettes sang at a lot of talent shows and worked at dances sponsored by a Detroit Disc Jockey known as Frantic Ernie Durham at a club on Detroit's west side called The Twenty Grand. While appearing at The Twenty Grand, The Primettes had a chance to meet all the big stars of the day, since the Club was a must-stop for any recording artists who came to Detroit.

After about a year of doing area talent shows and singing other artist's songs, the group decided to seek a recording contract. There were several record companies in Detroit and they tried them all, but one record company in particular was their prime target. A young man from Detroit had recently opened a record company and was receiving quite a bit of attention. The man's name was Berry Gordy, Jr. and his company was Motown.

You would think that The Primettes and Motown would make a perfect partnership, but that was not the case. After an audition, the girls were told they were too young to be making records.

Betty Travis was sixteen at the time, but the other girls were all thirteen or fourteen. The Primettes didn't give up their dream of working for Motown; instead they tried to get a second audition from a friend of Diane Ross. A young man named Bill Robinson lived down the street from Diane, and his group was already recording with Motown.

She pleaded with Smokey, as he was known (because of his love of westerns and the smoking gun fights), to intercede for her group. Smokey asked the girls to come to his fiancé's basement that night so he could hear them. After he evaluated their performance, he might talk to Berry Gordy about a second audition.

Mary Wilson recalls that audition very well: "We all met in Claudette's basement and Smokey and his whole group were there. We brought our guitar player, Marv Tarplin, along to accompany us. We sang several songs for Smokey, and when we were finished, the consensus was that we had great potential, but we should keep practicing and Smokey would see what he could do for us as far as a second audition. Smokey seemed quite impressed with our guitar player, Marv Tarplin. He asked Marv if he had any plans for the immediate future and when Marv said he didn't, Smokey asked him if he would like to join The Miracles as guitarist on an upcoming tour. Marv agreed, and in one night, we not only lost our guitarist, we still had no guarantee of a second audition."

The Primettes

clockwise from left: Barbara Martin, Diane Ross, Florence Ballard, Mary Wilson

That second auditition didn't go much better, but The Primettes were allowed to hang around the Motown studios. Eventually, Betty Travis decided to leave the group to get married. She was replaced by Barbara Martin, whom the girls all knew. She seemed to fit in nicely, so the change was uneventful.

As previously stated, the group was allowed to hang around the Motown studios until one day some backup singers were needed for a recording session. No one else was available, so it was decided that The Primettes would be used. Motown officials were impressed with their sound, so they began to use them as much as they could. Persistence had finally paid off; they were part of the Motown family, if only a small part. You must realize The Primettes were still in high school, so their aggressiveness is all the more impressive.

Finally, the big day came when Motown offered the four Primettes a contract. The salary offered them was minimal by today's standards, but it was a dream come true for the girls. It was this contract that altered The Primettes in a way that would make music history. Berry Gordy sent the girls word that he didn't care much for the name "Primettes". He told them to change their name to anything they wanted, but The Primettes was out. There was also a personnel change as well. Mary Wilson told me some interesting stories about the contract and the name change. "When we found out that Berry wanted our name changed, Florence started a list of names that we all liked. I must admit we liked The Primettes very much and we really didn't want to change our name. The name "Supremes" was added to the list by Florence, but we never thought we would use it.

The Supremes onstage
Photo Courtesy T.COX

Shortly after Berry asked us to change the name, we found out Barbara Martin's parents wouldn't let her sign the Motown contract. They wanted her to get a good steady job that was going to get her somewhere in the world. Music didn't strike them as a very secure business, so Barbara left the group. We all decided then and there that we might as well leave the group at three, because it seemed we were the only ones who would stick it out. That left us with only one problem-- our name. We still hadn't decided on a name when the day came to sign our contract. Florence had left our list of names at the Motown offices and when it came time to have the contract drawn up, the secretary who typed it up typed in the name Supremes. It wasn't our first choice, but from that day on we were know as The Supremes."

Success didn't come quickly for The Supremes. They did record regularly and did a lot of background work for other Motown artists in the studio , but they just couldn't get a hit.

It was kind of embarrassing for the girls because Motown records were selling like mad. Groups like the Marvelettes, Martha and the Vandellas, Marvin Gaye, and the girls' old friends, the Temptations, all had hit records out. Between 1961 and 1963, The Supremes released eight singles, none of which charted in the Top 40 positions of the Billboard Hot 100 . The Supremes didn't know it at the time, but they were being referred to as the "No Hit Supremes" around the Motown studios.

The one thing that kept the girls going was their dedication to the group. From the inception of The Primettes and later The Supremes, Diane, Flo and Mary worked for nothing else but the success of the group. During these years, all three members took turns singing lead: Wilson favored soft ballads; Ballard favored soulful, hard-driving songs with a bluesy edge ; and Ross favored mainstream pop songs. They would do whatever it took to make the group a success.

In 1963, after a string of failures, The Supremes finally hit the local charts with a song titled "When The Love Light Starts Shining Through His Eyes". Everyone at Motown thought this would get the girls off the ground, but unfortunately their next song bombed. The Motown hierarchy was determined to get the Supremes some exposure and as it turned out, Dick Clark was the man who gave it to them.

Clark wanted Brenda Holloway, one of Motown's top record sellers, to tour on his "Cavalcade of Stars". Brenda had one of the top songs in the nation at the time titled, "Every Little Bit Hurts". As part of the deal, Motown prevailed on Clark to take The Supremes with Brenda Holloway. They even offered to underwrite The Supremes' expenses if Clark would take them along on the tour. That was too good an offer to pass up, so Clark took it as he needed an opening act anyway. The Supremes were added to the tour. Mary Wilson remembers certain events on that tour that changed The Supremes almost overnight: "We were opening the show on Dick Clark's tour and we were about one quarter of the way through the tour when Motown released a song of ours titled "Where Did Our Love Go." By the end of the tour," Where Did Our Love Go" was the number one song in the nation, and we were Dick Clark's star attraction."

Berry Gordy knew that he should strike while the iron was hot. He released an album of old Supremes material titled *Meet The Supremes*. It was a collection of previously released Supremes music, but the album did relatively well sales-wise.

Gordy saw the potential in The Supremes and he put his finest writers, Brian and Eddie Holland and Lamont Dozier, to work on some songs for them . A second album was released in 1964 titled *Where Did Our Love Go.* From this album, two songs were released as singles and went to number one, "Baby Love" and "Come See About Me".

The Supremes were off and running, and with them went a string of Motown acts. Motown was selling records and their performers were very popular. Berry Gordy wanted his acts to work major night spots and national television shows. The Supremes were his ticket into every door he wanted to open. Soon after the release of The Supremes' second album, the company was deluged with offers for them . Topping the list was The Ed Sullivan Show, where the girls were a smash. Soon Ed Sullivan was using all of the Motown acts. The same can be said for American Bandstand. Incredible pressure was being put on The Supremes and they held up very well. They had an overwhelming concert schedule, television appearances, and of course their recording sessions were a must. It seemed that they were kept busy twenty four hours a day, but as I stated earlier, the girls were totally committed to Motown and The Supremes. More and more, Diana Ross, as she was now being called, was the primary voice and spokesperson for the group. She had a smile that dazzled everyone that met her and a personality to match.

Florence Ballard, who had a very rich and full voice in her own right, felt that she and Mary were becoming backup singers for Diana, which they were. She started protesting to Motown, and she was politely told not to make any waves. The company didn't care much for troublemakers and she knew that well. Flo had seen numerous personnel changes in various Motown groups, and she knew it could happen to her, as well, so she tried to keep the peace.

Many projects were in the works to move Diana Ross out of the group and on her own, when Florence started to balk once again. Flo was not at all happy that the group's pay structure had changed in favor of Diana, and she made mo secret of her displeasure. She started missing recording sessions, and rehearsals and gained quite a bit of weight. This didn't make her any friends with Motown management; they tried to go along with her because she was part of the company's number one act, and they felt she might come around with a little Tender Loving Care. In 1967 the rift between Florence and Motown reached its peak. She failed to appear at several engagements, and Mary and Diana had to work alone. Motown press releases claimed Florence was too ill to appear, but while they were issuing these statements to the press, the process of finding a replacement was already in the works.

Nobody can confidently state the exact reason for Flo's departure from The Supremes, but Mary Wilson told me her thoughts on what soured Flo on Motown: "I don't think Flo really understood that we were part of a big business. A lot of decisions concerning us were being made from purely a business angle. She thought we would always be the same three kids who started out together in 1959. Flo just couldn't accept the fact that our success was being geared around Diana. The fact was that our success was in great part due to Diana's appeal and that's the way The Supremes were being presented."

Cindy Birdsong, who had been singing with Patti LaBelle and the Bluebelles as a backup singer, was hired to replace Florence. She resembled Flo quite a lot and she blended well with Mary and Diana, so the change was uneventful. The company press releases stated that Flo had left the group to seek new career opportunities. The fact was she wanted out, and Motown was glad to see her go.

The personnel changes accomplished, the next test would be with The Supremes' new release. Holland, Dozier, and Holland took care of that with a song titled "Reflections". It was a hit for the girls, and the transition had been made without missing a beat. It was at this time that the group's name had a bit of a change. As I stated earlier, Berry Gordy's master plan was for Diana Ross to have a solo career. With that in mind, Gordy renamed the group Diana Ross and the Supremes. He felt that with her name out front, The Supremes, and Diana in particular, would get the recognition he thought they should have.

Berry Gordy worked overtime trying to get The Supremes more and more exposure. They appeared in a Tarzan episode, hosted a Hollywood Palace, and finally got a Special of their very own for N.B.C. titled "Taking Care Of Business".

Along with The Supremes, The Temptations, the top male group at Motown, were on the NBC Special. For their efforts, they were both invited to try another special the following year. The title of that special was "Getting Together on Broadway", which featured The Supremes and The Temptations singing their way through an hour of Broadway standards. This special showed off Diana Ross's true stage presence. In later years, this presence would lead her into a very successful acting career.

With the type of exposure The Supremes were getting, especially Diana, it wasn't long before the inevitable solo career of Diana Ross would become a reality. The split had been carefully orchestrated right from the beginning, and when the group recorded "Someday We'll Be Together" in 1969, it was decided that this would be the last song as a Supreme for Diana Ross.

A very elaborate farewell tour was mapped out and a successor to Diana was picked. It would be Jean Terrell, who had been singing with her brother's group Ernie Terrell and The Knockouts. Mary Wilson recalls that final tour: "Cindy and I knew that Diana would be leaving, but it was still a surprise when the final decision was made. I was very satisfied being a member of The Supremes, but Diana's goals were much greater. We had some success after Diana left, but it was never the same for The Supremes."

The group's final appearance was scheduled for The Frontier Hotel in Las Vegas in 1969. It was to be quite an event. A live album was to be recorded, and Dina's replacement, Jean Terrell, was to be introduced to the world. As everyone smiled and took a final bow, it was obvious that a fabulous era in music history was coming to an end. Added to this was a lawsuit by former Supreme Florence Ballard, who claimed she was still owed money by Motown. Eventually the lawsuit was settled, but it was discovered that, at Florence's untimely death in 1976, she was broke and living on welfare with her three children in a rundown neighborhood in Detroit--not a very attractive picture for a former member of the top female recording group of all time.

By the late seventies, The Supremes had been completely disbanded, with only their great memories left. I asked Mary Wilson to sum up The Supremes' chapter of this book. The following remarks seemed a perfect summation: "Being a member of The Supremes was like a dream come true for me. I felt very privileged to represent the city of Detroit wherever we traveled in the world. I also feel very privileged to think I helped to create and perpetuate The Motown Sound. Even though The Supremes are gone, the Motown Sound will live on forever in music history. My dreams never stopped. I will always be a Supreme and that suits me just fine. "

UPDATE: * In 1982, around the time that Motown reunited all of The Temptations, it was rumored that Motown would reunite The Supremes. The 1974 line-up of The Supremes (Wilson, Birdsong and Payne) was considered for this reunion, which was to include new recordings and a tour. Under advisement from Berry Gordy, Wilson declined to reunite, and the idea was scrapped. Ross briefly reunited with Wilson and Birdsong to perform "Someday We'll Be Together" on the Motown 25 television special, taped on March 25, 1983, and broadcast on NBC on May 16, 1983.

In 2000, plans were made for Ross to join Wilson and Birdsong for a planned "Diana Ross & the Supremes: Return to Love" reunion tour. However, Wilson passed on the idea, because while the promoters offered Ross $15 million to perform, Wilson was offered $4 million and Birdsong less than $1 million.] Ross herself offered to double the amounts both Wilson and Birdsong had originally been offered, but while Birdsong accepted, Wilson remained adamant, and as a result the deal fell through with both former Supremes. Eventually, the "Return to Love" tour went on as scheduled, but with Payne and Laurence joining Ross, although none of the three had ever been in the group at the same time and neither Payne nor Laurence had sung on any of the original hit recordings that they were now singing live. Susaye Greene was also considered for this tour, but refused to audition for it. The music critics cried foul and many fans were disappointed by both this and the show's high ticket prices. Thus, after playing only half of the dates on the itinerary, the tour was canceled.

* Detroit Free Press-Wikipedia

28. R. Dean Taylor

R. Dean Taylor

R. Dean Taylor was a young Canadian who came to Detroit from Toronto seeking his fame and fortune with Motown Records.

He arrived at Motown with an armload of songs he had written, and the Motown hierarchy was so impressed with his work that they signed him to a contract with their Rare Earth label. Motown was very much in the market for white entertainers for the Rare Earth label, so it seemed to be the perfect marriage.

Taylor wrote several songs which other Motown acts recorded, but in 1970 he wrote and recorded a song which would be his one and only hit with Motown. That song was titled "Indiana Wants Me", and the song climbed the charts and sold nearly 1 1/2 million records. Taylor continued recording for Rare Earth and working as a writer/producer for other artists until Rare Earth was ended during 1976. Though he never again scored the charts as he had done with "Indiana Wants Me", his releases did moderately well, especially in Canada. As a Canadian citizen, he could be played on CKLW and other Canadian radio stations and counted towards the stations Canadian content quotas. Taylor never reached those lofty heights again with Motown, and eventually left the company.

Taylor at 20 Grand with Holland and Dozier

UPDATE:

Taylor attempted a comeback during the early 1980s, after which he had a hiatus from the music industry. He has recently established his own record company, Jane Records.

Temptation Reunion photo 1982
Back Row: Dennis Edwards,
Eddie Kendricks, David Ruffin,
Melvin Franklin, Otis Williams
Front Row: Richard Street,
Glenn Leonard

29. The Temptations

From L to R :Melvin Franklin
David Ruffin
Otis Williams
Paul Williams
Eddie Kendricks
Photo Courtesy EDWARD PATTEN

They rose from the ghetto to become one of the most imitated singing groups in the world.

They have sung under such names as The Distants, The Primes, The Elgins, The Pirates and The Voicemasters, but the world knows them best as The Temptations. The original members of the group were Otis Williams, Paul Williams, Melvin Franklin, Elbridge (Al) Bryant and Eddie Kendricks.

This group was formed from two separate groups who were singing around Detroit in the late 50's. Eddie Kendricks and Paul Williams were part of a group known as The Primes and Bryant, Franklin and Otis Williams were with a group known as Otis Williams and The

Distants. It was a chance meeting at a neighborhood party where Williams and Kendricks first met and decided to merge their respective groups. Eddie Kendricks remembers that meeting quite clearly: "Our groups were quite aware of each other from various talent shows we had been in, and when we met at a party, we began to talk about our groups. As it turned out, we were both in the process of making some changes in our respective groups, so we decided to merge them into one. The real turning point came when Otis told me Berry Gordy of Motown Records had auditioned his group and told him to come back when the revisions in the group were made. Our ultimate goal was to get a recording contract, and when we signed with Motown, it was a dream come true. The new lineup of Otis Williams, Melvin Franklin, Elbridge "Al" Bryant, Eddie Kendricks, and Paul Williams took on the name The Elgins and auditioned for Motown in March 1961.

In the early days at Motown, Berry Gordy wrote and produced most of The Temptations' material. It wasn't until Smokey Robinson, an old high school friend of the group who also was with Motown, began writing and producing The Temptations material, that things started to happen for the group. Robinson produced a song entitled "I Want A Love I Can See", which became a regional hit for The Temptations. He followed that tune with another, "The Way You Do The Things You Do", which gave the group the national exposure they needed.

The original Temptations
From L to R: Eddie Kendricks
Melvin Franklin
Al Bryant
Otis Williams
Paul Williams
Photo Courtesy R.ASHFORD-HOLMES

It was at this time that a personnel change was made that would not only revamp the group, but its singing style, as well. A young man who had been traveling with The Temptations as a drummer, David Ruffin, replaced Elbridge Bryant in the group.

Ruffin had recorded as a solo artist with Chess Records, so he had the background Motown was looking for in a replacement. Bryant had not been getting along with Paul Williams, and when it became obvious that the continuity of the group was at stake, the change was made. That move gave The Temptations a singer who had a distinctive singing style, as well as great charisma.

Ruffin recalls his move from the background to the front man: "I had recorded several songs as a solo act with Chess Records, and when I came to Motown, I hoped something would open up for me. I never realized the success I would enjoy as a member of The Temptations. Joining the group was the best move of my career. "

With Ruffin singing lead and Smokey Robinson writing and producing for the group, The Temptations began to acquire star status with such hits as, "My Girl", (their first # 1 Song) , "It's Growing", "Beauty's Only Skin Deep" and "Ain't Too Proud To Beg".

The Temptations became quite an attraction in the entertainment world due not only to their singing, but also to their choreography. It was as much a treat to watch The Temptations and their precision-like choreography, as it was to hear them. They worked hard and long with Motown choreographer, the famous dancer Cholly Atkins, to refine their act. To this very day, other acts copy the "Temptation Walk", which was a distinguishing feature of their performance.

Bass singer Melvin Franklin recalls those hard hours under Aitkin's guidance: "When we went to Motown, one thing our group had going for us was our raw talent. Berry Gordy formed Motown's Artist Development Department so the acts could have their rough edges removed. We had always used some sort of choreography in our act, but it was rather crude compared to the precision steps Cholly Atkins taught us. We all felt very fortunate to have such an experienced instructor, so we put as much time and effort into our choreography as time would allow."

Eventually other groups began to use choreography in their own acts, but due to The Temptations' hard work and Cholly Aitkin's innovations, no one ever was able to quite capture The Temptations' style.

1968 proved to be a pivotal year for The Temptations. They were riding an amazing crest of popularity with such releases as "I Wish It Would Rain" and "I Could Never Love Another After Loving You", with David Ruffin singing the lead. In addition, Motown was in the process of creating new names for their major groups who had distinctive singing styles, such as Diana Ross and The Supremes, Smokey Robinson and The Miracles, and Martha Reeves and The Vandellas. David Ruffin took advantage of this and went to Berry Gordy with the idea that The Temptations should be renamed David Ruffin and The Temptations. To all appearances, David had already set himself above the rest of the group. He traveled separately when they were on the road, in a private car. He had his own valet to care for his personal needs. Then he began to miss rehearsals and singing engagements in an effort to force Motown to grant him star status. After he missed an engagement in Cleveland, Ohio in 1968, the other members of the group decided life would be a lot simpler without him, so they informed Berry Gordy that David Ruffin had to go.

As I stated earlier, Motown wouldn't hesitate to remove a troublesome singer from any group, so in 1968, David Ruffin found himself a solo artist once again. Dennis Edwards, who had been singing with The Contours, was brought in to replace Ruffin. To add insult to injury, The Temptations' first release with Edwards singing lead was the top ten hit "Cloud Nine". David didn't take his expulsion well. He would show up at Temptation engagements and try to join the group on stage. The problem got so bad that Motown had to hire extra security people to keep David away from the stage. Eventually, Ruffin got his solo career into high gear with the release of his top ten hit, "My Whole World Ended The Moment You Left Me", and a peaceful coexistence began between The Temptations and David Ruffin.

The Temptations

The group continued to record and tour quite successfully, and a new horizon beckoned when they were asked to co-star with Diana Ross and The Supremes in an hour long prime time television special on NBC, "Taking Care Of Business." Both groups appeared on numerous television shows, but only for one or two songs. This was to be the first time any Motown group would be spotlighted in their own special. A combination group comprised of The Supremes and The Temptations released an album from that TV show titled *T.C.B;* from that album came a number two hit titled "I'm Gonna Make You Love Me".

Everything seemed to be going fine for The Temptations as they entered the 70's. They continued to release hit songs such as "Runaway Child",

" I Can't Get Next To You", and "Psychedelic Shack", but the tremendous work load and traveling schedule began to take its toll on Paul Williams.

Paul had taken a leadership role in the group since its inception, also aiding Cholly Atkins with the group's choreography. The pressures began to pile up, and in 1971 Paul Williams, being near total exhaustion, was told by doctors to curtail his workload. It was decided Paul would no longer tour with the group, although he would still record and work as their choreographer. Richard Street was brought in from another Motown group known as The Monitors to replace Paul, who was having marital and financial problems as well. As for the group, things were going well. Their release of "Just My Imagination" hit number one on the charts and earned The Temptations a Grammy Award.

It also marked the exit of Eddie Kendricks from the group. Eddie's voice was the lead on "Just My Imagination" and following its tremendous reception, Eddie sought a solo career. Kendricks explains how his solo career came about: "When my contract with Motown ran out, I was approached by several rival companies about a solo career. Every artist thinks about a solo career, and I was no exception. I had nothing against the group or Motown; it was strictly a business decision. The contract I signed served as a security blanket for my future."

Eddie Kendricks was replaced by Damon Harris and The Temptations continued to record with even more success. They were awarded another Grammy for "Papa Was A Rollin' Stone", and it seemed that no matter how many personnel changes occurred, The Temptations would stay on top.

In 1973, tragedy struck The Temptations at a very personal level. Paul Williams, the heart and soul of the group since its inception, facing numerous personal and financial problems, committed suicide. His body was found in his car just two blocks from Motown's original studios. Otis Williams recalls how the group reacted to the tragic news: "It was probably the most disappointing thing that happened to us as a group. We knew Paul was having problems, but I guess we never knew how bad a time he was really having. He never got over not being able to perform with us and that was probably the worst thing that could have happened to Paul. All he ever lived for was to be a Temptation, and when he couldn't perform with us any longer, he never really felt part of the group again."

Paul's oldest and closest friend, Eddie Kendricks, put his death in a beautiful perspective. "Paul was the chemistry that made our group work. He was the catalyst for our choreography and the glue which held us together when times got tough. Wherever any of The Temptations go, a little bit of Paul Williams will go with us."

This brings us to the time Motown left for California, and The Temptations were a big part of that move. After *The Temptations Do the Temptations* was recorded in 1976, Edwards was fired from the group, and with new lead Louis Price on board, they left Motown for Atlantic Records. It proved to be a bad move, and it took nearly two years of litigation for The Temptations to get our of their contract. In the interim, their careers were on hold. Success continued to elude the group at Atlantic, however. Their two releases on Atlantic -- *Hear To Tempt You*(1977) and *Bare Back* (1978)-- along with their associated singles, had failed to perform any better at Atlantic than their last handful of singles had at Motown. As a result, in 1979 Atlantic released the group from its contract. Shortly afterwards, The Temptations met once again with Smokey Robinson and Berry Gordy, who re-signed the group to Motown in 1980 where they remain today (1982), the most popular soul group of all time.

Members:

Otis Williams
Ron Tyson
Terry Weeks
Joe Herndon
Bruce Williamson

Past Members:

Elbridge "Al" Bryant
Melvin Franklin
Eddie Kendricks
Paul Williams
David Ruffin
Dennis Edwards
Ricky Owens

Richard Street
Damon Harris
Glenn Leonard
Louis Price
Ali-Ollie Woodson
Theo Peoples
Ray Davis
Harry McGilberry
Barrington "Bo" Henderson
G. C. Cameron

UPDATE:* The Temptations were inducted into the Vocal Group Hall of Fame in 1999. In 2001, their 2000 album *Ear-Resistible* won the group its third Grammy, this one for Best Traditional R&B Vocal Performance. Bo Henderson was fired from the group in 2003, prompting a wrongful termination lawsuit. His replacement was former Spinners lead G. C. Cameron. The lineup of Cameron, Otis Williams, Ron Tyson, Harry McGilberry, and Terry Weeks recorded for a short time before Harry McGilberry was dismissed; his replacement was former Spaniels bass Joe Herndon . McGilberry died on April 3, 2006, at age 56.

The group's final Motown album, *Legacy* , was released in 2004. Later that year, The Temptations asked to be released from their Motown contract, and moved to another Universal Motown Music Group label, New Door Records. Their sole album with this lineup, *Reflections*, was released on January 31, 2006, and contains covers of several popular Motown songs, including Diana Ross & the Supremes' "Reflections", the Miracles' "Ooo Baby, Baby", Marvin Gaye and Tammi Terrell's "Ain't Nothing Like The Real Thing", and The Jackson 5's "I'll Be There". In 2005, The Temptations were inducted into the Michigan Rock and Roll Legends Hall of Fame. In 2007, The Temptations' recording of "My Girl" was voted a Legendary Michigan Song. The Temptations were nominated for the 2007Grammy Award for Best Traditional R&B Vocal, for their version of Gaye's "How Sweet It Is (To Be Loved By You)" from *Reflections*.

G. C. Cameron left the group in June 2007 to focus on his solo career. He was replaced by new member Bruce Williamson. The new lineup recorded another album of soul covers, *Back to Front*, released in October 2007. Former member Ali-Ollie Woodson died on May 30, 2010 after a long battle with leukemia.

On May 4, 2010, the group released their *Still Here* album. A song featured, "First Kiss", has been criticized for having usages of Auto-Tune.

As of 2010, the Temptations continue to perform and record for Universal Records with its one living original member, Otis Williams, still in the lineup.

*Wikipedia

146

30. Tammi Terrell

Tammi Terrell

The story of Tammi Terrell (Thomasina Winifred Montgomery) is one of the most tragic among those entertainers who worked for Motown.

She was struck down by a fatal brain tumor at the peak of her career when she was 25 years old.

Tammi came to Motown after having worked with Steve Gibson and The Red Capps and The James Brown Revue. After recording a single for Checker Records in 1964,paired with singer Jimmy Radcliffe on a now-released duet version of the song "If I Would Marry You", Terrell semi-retired from show business and enrolled in the University of Pennsylvania where she stayed for two years, majoring in pre-med.

In 1965, Jerry "The Ice Man " Butler asked Terrell to sing with him in a series of nightclub shows, which Terrell agreed to with a schedule that would allow her to continue her studies in Pennsylvania. In March 1965, Motown CEO Berry Gordy spotted Terrell performing in Detroit at The Twenty Grand Club and asked her to sign with Motown. Terrell agreed and signed with Motown on April 29, 1965, her 20th birthday.

The management people at Motown saw Tammi's potential were elated that she signed up. The fact that she worked for James Brown certainly helped. It was a well know fact that James Brown was a perfectionist who only worked with people who were very disciplined. These were the traits all record companies looked for in an artist.

Motown released two singles on Tammi, "Come On And See Me", and "I Don't Believe You Love Me" that were only marginally successful. It was at this time that Motown executive Harvey Fuqua decided to team Tammi with Marvin Gaye on a duet. Marvin had recorded successful duets with both Mary Wells and Kin Weston early in their careers, with good results. Fuqua hoped that lightning would strike once again with Tammi.

Not only did lightning strike, but the team of Gaye and Terrell lit up the sky with five straight hit songs. "Ain't No Mountain High Enough", "Your Precious Love", "If I Could Build My Whole World Around You", "Ain't Nothing Like The Real Thing", and "You're All I Need To Get By" were all top twenty hits and it seemed their success would go on forever. Gaye and Terrell's first duet album, *United*, was released in the late summer of 1967. Throughout that year, Gaye and Terrell began performing together, Terrell became a vocal and performance inspiration for the shy and laid-back Gaye, who hated live performing. The duo even performed together on television to showcase their hits.

Their success came to an end one tragic night in Cleveland in 1968. While performing a song, Tammi collapsed on stage and Marvin rushed out to catch her before she fell. Gaye continued the show while Tammi was taken to the hospital for tests. It was believed she was suffering from exhaustion and fatigue, but it was later discovered that she was suffering from a brain tumor. She underwent several delicate operations to remove the tumor, but for all practical purposes, her performing career was over. The illness had quite an effect on Marvin, as well. It was quite some time before he was able to resume his concert schedule.

During my research on Tammi's chapter I kept uncovering a popular rumor as to how Tammi came to acquire the brain tumor she suffered from. It is said that she suffered a beating at the hands of a fellow Motown singer with whom she was involved. It is also said that, shortly after this beating, Tammi began to suffer from terrible headaches. It was further rumored that this particular entertainer was forced to leave Motown shortly after Tammi's death. In all honesty, I was unable to substantiate any of these rumors, but because the rumors surfaced several times, I thought I should address them if for no other reason than to put an end to them.

After several operations to correct the tumor, Tammi seemed well on her way to a favorable recovery; then, shortly before her 25th birthday, Tammi Terrell died quite unexpectedly. It is believed that she died from complications resulting from the tumor. Tammi died much too young, as did a number of other talented Motown people. She did, however, leave behind the legacy of her music for her many fans.

UPDATE:

At the funeral, Gaye delivered a final eulogy. According to Terrell's fiancé, who was also friends with Gaye, Terrell's mother allowed Gaye at the funeral but told him that Terrell's other Motown colleagues would not be allowed in. Terrell's mother criticized Motown for not helping with Terrell's illness, accusing the label of covering up the singer's condition, and releasing albums of Terrell's work without her consent. Gaye had also contended that he felt Motown was taking advantage of Terrell's illness and refused to promote the *Easy* album, despite Motown telling him it would cover Terrell's health expenses. Gaye never fully got over Terrell's death, according to friends, and several biographers stated Terrell's death led Gaye to descend into depression and substance abuse.

On October 8, 2010, Hip-O-Select released *Come On And See Me: The Complete Solo Collection*, a compilation of all of Terrell's solo work dating back to high school, plus never before released songs and 13 minutes of the only known live stage recordings.

31. Willie Tyler & Lester

Willie Tyler & Lester
in early Motown publicity photo
Photo Courtesy T. COX

Willie Tyler and Lester were quite unlike most of the entertainers that worked at Motown Records. They were not recording stars and, except for an occasional comedy album, they didn't record at all.

Willie Tyler was a ventriloquist and Lester was his dummy. They were discovered working at a summer resort in Idyllwild, Michigan by a Motown executive who encouraged Willie to audition at one of Motown's Wednesday morning talent hunts. When Motown saw Willie's act, they jumped at the chance to hire a performer who would be a prefect opening act for the musical acts at Motown. Before Willie and Lester, there were usually two musical acts booked together. Hiring the ventriloquist provided balance to Motown shows.

Willie worked with virtually every act at Motown, and he attained experience that would prove valuable to him in the future. "When the Motown Revues would work at the Fox Theater in Detroit, the audience was usually made up of young people. The Fox would book the shows during Christmas vacation so the kids were out of school. I used to get a lot of heckling from the kids, but with Lester being able to answer them back, it kept the audience happy and provided me with a lot of experience."

Working with one of the top record companies in the world was like a dream come true for Willie Tyler. He was born and raised in Detroit and attended school not far from the Motown studios. It was while he was growing up in Detroit that his interest in ventriloquism began. "I used to watch Paul Winchell and Jerry Mahoney. I got a doll and practiced every day with it. I finally started entering talent shows when I was in high school, but it wasn't until I went into the Army and did shows for the Special Services that I decided to go into show business for a living."

Today, Willie is one of the top ten ventriloquists in the business. He and Lester work major night spots all over the world. They appear regularly on television as well as in commercials. He resides in California with his wife and children, and of course, Lester.

Willie informed me there was a Lester doll on the market now and I couldn't help but wonder if there was some young boy or girl out there practicing their technique on a Lester doll. I suppose we should keep our eyes open.

UPDATE: * He got his first big break in 1972 on Rowan & Martin's Laugh-In. He is the father of Tarince Tyler, and actor Cory Tyler .

Tyler has had guest roles in *The Parent Hood, Pacific Blue, The White Shadow* and *The Jeffersons* , as well as serving as host of the popular Saturday morning children's anthology series, *The ABC Weekend Special* throughout the early 1980s. He also appeared in the 1978 movie, *Coming Home*. He appeared as himself in the 2004 BET Comedy Awards, *For Da Love of Money*, the 4th Annual Black Gold Awards, The 1st Annual Soul Train Awards , *Motown Returns to the Apollo, Lou Rawls Parade of Stars, American Bandstand , Vegetable Soup, The Flip Wilson Show* , and *The Hollywood Palace*. On September 18, 2006, Tyler was the first ventriloquist to appear on the *Late Show with David Letterman*'s Ventriloquist Week.

* Wikipedia

32. The Underdogs

The Underdogs

The Underdogs were a group of suburban high school teenagers who enjoyed tremendous success in various teen clubs around Detroit. The Underdogs were a four-man garage band from Grosse Pointe, MI, with a lineup similar to the Beatles -- three guitars and a drum-- manned by Dave Whitehouse (vocals/bass), Tony Roumell (lead guitar/vocals), Chris Lena (rhythm guitar/vocals), and Michael Morgan (drums/vocals).

Berry Gordy, being ever vigilant in his ongoing quest for Detroit area talent, signed them to a contract in hopes of adding to his growing artist pool. The Underdogs were very much part of the Motown family, although their backgrounds were quite different from the other Motown groups. For the most part, they were raised in a rather well-to-do environment and formed their group more for fun than anything else. This does not detract from their efforts and the hard work they put into their music. If Motown signed them, they had talent!

The bands' hometown popularity had piqued the interest of Motown Records . They had one single release on the *VIP* label, a tough-as-nails makeover of Holland-Dozier-Holland's "Love's Gone Bad" originally done by blue-eyed soul-singer Chris Clark. The Underdogs are reportedly the first white band signed by Motown, but that's debatable, with "band" being the key word. There were white acts before the advent of The Underdogs.

What should have been a hit didn't generate much chart action according to Motown's standards, reaching its zenith at number 122 on the pop charts in 1966.

The Underdogs at The Hideout with friends

The group had a lot of appeal due to their clean-cut, good looks, but unfortunately, Motown was unable to present them as part of "The Motown Sound". People expected black artists coming out of Motown, and the few white acts, such as The Underdogs, never attained the popularity the black acts did. They cut other unreleased singles at Motown including a blistering version of "The Way You Do the Things You Do" that was shelved for years, but can now be found on compilation albums such as *Motown Sings Motown* and others.

The Underdogs did have several tunes released while at Motown, with the most popular being "The Man In The Glass". They toured occasionally with the Motortown Revue, but since they were teenagers, they eventually broke up and sought their fortunes in safer waters outside of the music industry.

33. The Valadiers

The Valadiers hold the distinction of being the first white group Motown Records signed to a contract. Stuart Avig, Jerry Light, Marty Coleman and Art Glasser were white Jewish kids known as The Valadiers. Following the advice of their idol Jackie Wilson, The Valadiers auditioned for Berry Gordy, hoping to land a contract with his newly formed company.

When The Valadiers walked in for the audition, their chances seemed slim to none as Berry was looking for that unique sound of soul and did not expect that from four white faces. Gordy was quite impressed with their harmony, however; it was decided that they did indeed have the sound that Gordy was looking for, and he signed them to a contract.

A lot has been made about The Valadiers being the first white group signed by Motown, but the fact was, most of the singers Berry Gordy knew were black, so those were the singers he recruited. The Valadiers released several tunes during their stay at Motown, the most popular being, "Greetings, This Is Uncle Sam." The Valadiers' next recordings appeared on the Gordy label, "When I'm Away", "Because I Love Her" and "I Found a Girl". These songs were hits, but none were as successful as

"Greetings". By 1964 The Valadiers disbanded and lead singer Stuart Avig went on to pursue a solo career. Stuart cut 2 solo tracks at Golden World Records as Stuart Ames, "King For A Day" and "Oh Angelina".

Ironically, the group was forced to break up because their lead singer was drafted in 1962, and they were never able to replace him.

UPDATE

In 1989 British music producer Ian Levine came to Detroit to record all of the old Motown stars, including The Valadiers. Stuart Avig was the sole original member along with his current group, The Latin Counts. The Valadiers recorded numerous tracks that included remakes of the Spinners' "Love Don't Love Nobody," The Isley Brothers "I Guess I'll Always Love You," as well as "Behind A Painted Smile", "No Competition", "What's Wrong With Me Baby" and "Truth Hurts". Stuart sounded as good as ever!

In 2002 Stuart Avig joined forces with The Shades of Blue who recorded the chartbuster "Oh How Happy". The Shades of Blue along with Stuart have performed all over the country for the past 9 years. In 2009 Motown Records celebrated its 50th Anniversary and after numerous requests from promoters, artists and fans The Valadiers got back together for one last run. Original lead singer Stuart Avig has joined forces with Andy Alonzo (who has been a Valadier since 1980), Donald Revels and Charlie Valverde.

34. The Vancouvers

Bobby Taylor and The Vancouvers have one of the most interesting stories at Motown. They were, for the most part, a group which would open the show for most of the major acts at Motown. They were also a mainstay of the Motor Town Revues, which toured the country.

If the group had a problem, it was that although they were great showmen, that showmanship couldn't be translated to their records. Gordy brought the Vancouvers to Motown Records and signed them to his Gordy Records imprint. By this time the evolving lineup consisted of Bobby Taylor, Wes Henderson and Tommy Chong along with guitarist Eddie Patterson, organist Robbie King, and drummer Duris Maxwell (aka Ted Lewis), the latter three having come as a package when the original Vancouvers merged with another local group, the Good Shepherds.

The Vancouvers only successfully released one song titled "Does Your Mother Know About Me?" This Tommy Chong co-composition peaked at number 29 on the Billboard Hot 100. Despite their lack of recording prowess, The Vancouvers' background is very interesting. A young man who was a part of the group and was a fine musician, would enjoy tremendous success in years to come recording comedy albums and making motion pictures. His name was Tommy Chong. I'm sure you have heard of Cheech and Chong, and now you know where he got his start.

The second story surrounding The Vancouvers centers around a concert at the Regal Theater in Chicago. Joining the group were four brothers from Gary, Indiana. At the time, they were know as The Little Jackson Brothers, and they stole the show. Bobby Taylor was so impressed what when he arrived back at Motown studios, he begged Berry Gordy to give The Jackson Brothers an audition. Gordy had a show scheduled for Gary, Indiana, so he booked the youngsters on the show and the rest is Motown history. Despite all the stories you have heard about Diana Ross discovering The Jacksons Five, it was actually Bobby Taylor.

Bobby Taylor and The Vancouvers may not be a household Motown name, but they were certainly among the most interesting on the Motown roster.

Past Members:

Bobby Taylor
Tommy Chong
Wes Henderson
Eddie Patterson
Robbie King
Ted Lewis

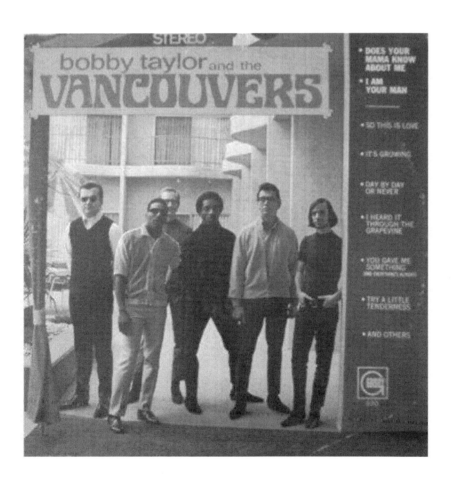

UPDATE * By1971, Taylor had departed Motown because of a financial dispute, recording sporadically into the mid-1970s.

Taylor later successfully sued Motown for a substantial amount of money. Moving to the United Kingdom, Taylor started an offshoot group, Bobby Taylor & the New Vancouvers, and recorded an album for Ian Levine's Motorcity Records. His later musical efforts were tempered by bouts with throat cancer, which he had treated by various holistic doctors. Despite that, the group's recording of a medley of The Original's *Baby I'm For Real* with *The Bells*, (a/k/a "The Bells I Hear"), found on the two-volume CD "Motown Sings Motown Treasures" has become increasingly popular.

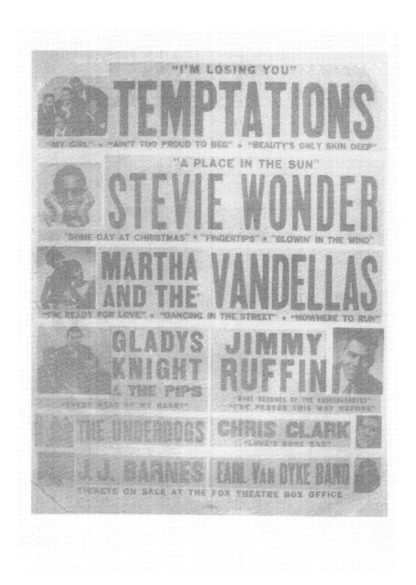

35. Martha & The Vandellas

THE VANDELLAS

Martha Reeves and The Vandellas were a of group that worked hard getting noticed; when they got their chance, they made the most of it. Theirs is the classic story of hard work and perseverance paying off with success.

Martha Reeves' musical career began right in her own home singing gospel music with her family. The first formal training Martha received came from a high school teacher she had in Detroit. "Mr. Silver at Northeastern High School was very influential in the training of my voice. He taught me how to use my God-given talents and encouraged me to join various choral groups at school. When I graduated in 1958, I was chosen to sing the lead in Bach's "Hallelujah", for a radio broadcast featuring our choral group. That was my first public appearance. "

Once out of high school, Martha was encouraged by her mother to pursue her singing career while working at Citywide Cleaning. She began singing the blues in various nightspots under the name Martha Lavaille. It was at this time she met Mickey Stephenson, who would be very instrumental in Martha joining Motown Records.

Martha was also singing with at group called The Del-Phi's, made up of Martha, Annette Beard, and Rosalind Ashford. Mr. Fred Brown saw the group one night and decided to take them under his wing. He was already managing the career of J. J. Barnes, who was quite an up-and- coming singer in the Detroit area. It was while Mr. Brown was handling The Del Phi's that they recorded a couple of songs for Chess Records. Although the records didn't sell very well, the experience gained by the group was invaluable.

British television special in 1964
Photo Courtesy T. COX

Mickey Stephenson entered the picture yet again. He was now the A & R director at Motown and remembered Martha from her days as Martha Lavaille. Mickey encouraged Martha to audition at Motown with a group known as The Mellowtones. Unfortunately, the audition was postponed, but Mickey asked Martha to stay on as his secretary until something came along for her musically.

Mickey Stevenson

Besides her secretarial duties, Martha recalls that her job encompassed much, much more: "When I first went to work for Motown, I worked the first three weeks for nothing. Finally after the third week a salary of $35.00 was agreed upon. Besides the usual secretarial duties, I found myself installing a system by which all of the musicians would be paid properly for their work. In the past, no records were kept and that resulted in a lot of squabbles over money. Another one of my duties was to listen to audition tapes and pass them along to the Motown executives. I was proud of the faith they showed in my judgment."

As will happen in any new business, people were asked to fill in wherever they were needed. That is how Martha made her way into the recording studio. She would be used occasionally to sing backup on various Motown recordings, but one day she was asked to sing lead on song destined for Mary Wells.

Mary was in the process of negotiating a new contract and couldn't record until the contract issue was settled. It was decided that Martha Reeves would sing lead on the song. Because the regular backup singers, The Andantes, were not available for this session, Martha contacted Rosalind Ashford and Annette Beard, who sang with Martha as The Delphis.

The tune was called, "I'll Have To Let Him Go". Berry Gordy was so pleased with the results of the session that he decided that Martha Reeves and her friends would record with Motown regularly. It should be noted that the flip side of "I'll Have To Let Him Go" was a tune written by Martha Reeves titled, "My Baby Won't Come Back".

Martha, Rosalind and Annette were renamed The Vells and began recording with various Motown projects. The Vells worked particularly well with Marvin Gaye, and could be heard on such tunes as "Stubborn Kind Of Fella", "Pride and Joy" and "Hitch Hike". Another name change came about as the group was renamed The Vandellas, and they began appearing with Marvin Gaye in his live performances.

While The Vandellas were in New York preparing for a show at the Apollo Theater with Marvin Gaye, Berry Gordy sent for them to come home and record a tune he had found for them. The title was "Come and Get These Memories"; with that song, Martha and The Vandellas were on their way. With Holland, Dozier, and Holland providing such hits as "Heat Wave" and "Quicksand", the group was in constant demand on night clubs, television and concerts. Their second hit, "Heat Wave", became a phenomenal record for the group, reaching number four on the Hot 100 and hitting number one on the R&B singles chart for five weeks.

It became their first million-seller and eventually won the group their only Grammy Award nomination for Best R&B Vocal Performance by a Duo or Group.

All of this fame left quite an impression on former Vandella Rosalind Ashford: "It seemed we were a busy group. I really shouldn't complain, because the reason we were kept busy was our records were selling quite well. Our music took us places we probably would have never gone. I have some very fond memories of our European tours, our appearances on The Ed Sullivan Show and our engagement at The Copa. Working at The Copa was my biggest thrill. At the time, it was the top nightclub in the country."

During the mid-sixties, Annette Beard left the Vandellas and was replaced by Betty Kelly. Betty had been singing with another Motown group known as The Velvellettes. Whenever Motown had to change personnel, it was never a problem. There was always a replacement available from their own ranks. Within the company there was a great deal of friendly competition. Martha Reeves told me there were a lot of misconceptions about her rivalry with Diana Ross: "A lot had been written about Diana and I not getting along. We pulled for each other's group to do well. After all, if one of us looked good, it made the other groups look good. I also feel we opened doors for each other. For example, we were very popular in Europe before The Supremes were, so when we went to on a tour of Europe, The Supremes went along. Those types of tours opened up all of Europe, for all of the Motown groups. Conversely, Diana and The Supremes got the first nightclub and television exposure for Motown, and those avenues opened up for the rest of us. We were really quite fond of each other and we respected each other's work. There will always be friendly competition between groups in a company such as Motown was."

More changes occurred with The Vandellas, as Betty Kelly left the group and was replaced by Martha Reeves' sister, Lois. The sound remained the same, and the group recorded such hits as "Nowhere To Run", "Jimmy Mack" and "I'm Ready For Love".

The group remained on tour for very long periods of time because of their popularity. One spot in particular was like a second home for Martha and The Vandellas: The Apollo Theater in New York. Rosalind Ashford had fond memories of those Apollo shows: "When we went to the east coast for a tour, the Apollo was a must. It seemed that we were always one of their top draws. Each time we would appear there, we would set new attendance records. It's always gratifying to sell out a show anywhere, but the Apollo always seemed to be a lucky charm for us".

In 1967, the City of Detroit was crippled by a devastating riot. The people at Motown were a very calming influence on the black community. In the forefront as peacemakers were Martha and The Vandellas. Disc jockeys all over town were playing their hit record, "Dancing In The Streets", in hopes the community would indeed dance, rather than riot.

Martha Reeves remembers exactly where the group was when the riots broke out: "We were onstage at the Fox Theater in Detroit, when word reached us that rioting had broken out. We had to stop the show and tell our audience to go home at once. From the show we were ushered to a local radio station, where we stayed on the radio for almost 24 hours straight. We took calls from listeners and spoke to the people of Detroit. I hope we did some good; the people of Detroit held us in high regard and I hope they listened to what we had to say."

By 1969 the last original Vandella, Rosalind Ashford, had left the group over a money dispute with Martha Reeves. She was replaced by Sandra Tilly, another former Velvellette. There were rumors that Martha Reeves would leave and do a solo act much as Diana Ross, but that never materialized. Shortly thereafter, Martha married and had a son. For all practical purposes, the group had reached the end of the road. Although Martha returned to the group shortly after her son was born, it became more and more tiresome for her to be on the road away from her family.

As 1970 arrived, Motown made the momentous decision to leave Detroit for California. Martha and The Vandellas were caught in the transition. Martha recalls that decision: " When Motown decided to leave for California, the transition was to be gradual. They were going to leave a certain amount of people behind to hold down the Detroit operation until the transition was completed. The producers they left behind couldn't capture the style we had established. We were used to Holland, Dozier and Holland material and the type of songs we were getting weren't that quality. Finally, when the final move was made, we were dropped from the roster, in favor of The Commodores. We hadn't had a hit in nearly three years and The Commodores were rising stars, so the decision was an easy one for Motown to make. "

Once her Motown days were over, Martha Reeves moved around to various record companies and producers, but none were able to capture the magic she enjoyed at Motown. A lot of producers worked with Martha, only to pick her brain about the inner workings of Motown. As you may recall Martha was involved at every level of Motown's operation, and many record companies tried to take advantage of her knowledge. Martha recalls those incidents: "A lot of people from other record companies thought that I would be so bitter with Motown that I would make **their** company another Motown out of spite. The one thing they didn't count on was my loyalty to Motown and to Berry Gordy. The one thing those companies didn't have was Berry Gordy running the show. To me he was a genius. Those other people were only pickpockets, trying to hitch their way to the top. I really resented them for that."

Today, Martha Reeves continues to perform as a solo act or with her sisters as a group. She sings at a lot of "oldies" shows and enjoys it very much. Despite some financial setbacks, Martha Reeves looks ahead to enjoying the success she knew in the 60's.

Her sister Lois, one of The Vandellas, is happily married and living in Detroit where she helps her husband run their lounge. She occasionally works with Martha in the Detroit area when the opportunity presents itself. Rosalind Ashford-Holmes, another of The Vandellas, is married and the mother of a son. She lives in Detroit and works for the phone company.

Martha and The Vandellas have established a list of hit songs that would make any group green with envy. Wherever people speak the name of the top singers of the rock era, the name Martha and The Vandellas will always be at the forefront.

Past Members:

Martha Reeves*
Rosalind Ashford-Holmes*
Annette Beard-Helton*
Gloria Williams* (deceased)
Betty Kelly
Lois Reeves
Sandra Tilley (deceased)
*Denotes original Members

UPDATE: *

Mickey Stevenson, Martha Reeves

When Motown went to California, Reeves did not want to move. She negotiated out of her deal with Motown, signing with MCA in 1974, and releasing the critically-acclaimed self-titled debut, *Martha Reeves*. Despite critical rave reviews of her work, neither of Reeves' post-Vandellas/Motown recordings produced the same success as they had the decade before. After living what she called "a rock & roll lifestyle" of prescription pills and alcohol, Reeves sobered up in 1977, overcoming her addictions and becoming a born-again Christian.

After the Vandellas' split, Reeves' sister Lois sang with the group Quiet Elegance and also sang background for Al Green. Sandra Tilley retired from show business in the late 1970s, suddenly dying of a brain aneurysm in 1981 at the age of thirty-nine. Original member Gloria Williams, who retired from show business when she left the group, died in 2000. In 1978, Reeves and original Vandellas Ashford and Beard-Sterling reunited at a Los Angeles benefit concert for actor Will Geer. In 1983, Reeves successfully sued for royalties from her Motown hits and the label agreed to have the songs credited as *Martha Reeves and the Vandellas* from then on. That year, Reeves performed solo at Motown 25 which, along with some of their songs being placed on the *Big Chill* soundtrack, helped Reeves and the Vandellas gain a new audience.

In 1989, original members Ashford and Sterling also sued Motown for royalties. During this, the original trio were inspired to reunite both as a recording act and in performances. They were offered a recording contract with Bob Dylan at Motorcity Records and issued the group's first single since the Vandellas disbanded seventeen years before, with "Step Into My Shoes".

From 2005 to 2009, Reeves held the eighth seat of Detroit's city council. In August, she lost her seat and told the press that she would continue performing.

Except for pre-Vandellas member Gloria Williamson, all members of the group were inducted into the Rock & Roll Hall of Fame in 1995, becoming the second all-female group to be so honored , and were presented with the induction by rock group The B-52's, whose frothy dance music was inspired by the Vandellas. They were also inducted to the Vocal Group Hall of Fame in 2003. Two of their singles, "(Love Is Like a) Heat Wave" and "Dancing in the Street" were included in the list of The Rock and Roll Hall of Fame's 500 Songs that Shaped Rock and Roll.

In 2004, Rolling Stone Magazine ranked the group #96 on their list of the 100 Greatest Artists of All Time. In 2005, Martha & The Vandellas were inducted into the Michigan Rock and Roll Legends Hall of Fame. "Dancing In The Street" was voted a Legendary Michigan Song in 2008.

In July 2010, Reeves returned to the studio and recorded new tracks by Swedish producer Soren Jensen and her long-time musical director, Al McKenzie. She was recently asked how long she would continue as a performer to which Reeves replied: "I'm going to sing as long as I'm able; I'm going to dance as long as I can. And age 69 feels real good." She also recently expressed dismay at the state of current pop music, saying, "We didn't have to send our children out of the room when we were with Motown. Our songs have always been about love, happiness, joy and partying."

Martha Reeves headlined at the 2011 Smithsonian Folklife Festival in Washington D.C. on July 1 as part of the R&B Program.

36. The Velvelettes

The Velvellettes

The Velvelettes were the type of group that looked like a hundred other female groups during the 60's, just three girls singing upbeat material about love and their boyfriends. The group was founded in 1961 by Bertha Barbee McNeal and Mildred Gill Arbor, students at Western Michigan University. Mildred recruited her younger sister Carolyn (also known as Cal or Caldin), who was in 9th grade, and Cal's friend Betty Kelley, a junior in high school. Bertha brought along her cousin Norma Barbee, a freshman at Flint Junior College. Cal was chosen as the group's lead singer.

A classmate at Western Michigan University, Robert Bullock, was Berry Gordy's nephew, and he encouraged the group to audition for Motown Records. The group signed to Motown in late 1962 and started recording in January 1963.

The group had one sizable hit, "Needle In A Haystack", but for the most part they were relegated to opening act status for the major groups at Motown. The Velvelettes got their break chart-wise in the spring of 1964 thanks to young producer Norman Whitfield, who produced "Needle In A Haystack" as a single for the group on Motown's VIP Records imprint. "Needle In A Haystack" peaked at number 45 on the Billboard Hot 100 in mid-1964. The group recorded its follow-up, "He Was Really Sayin' Something" , with Whitfield again producing, and spent time on Motown-sponsored tours as a support act. In September 1964, after recording

"Dancing In The Street" earlier in June, Betty Kelly officially left the group to join Martha and The Vandellas, and the quintet became a quartet.

There is a very interesting side note to The Velvelettes that has to do with The Vandellas. Two of their members were brought in to replace members of the Vandellas, Betty Kelly and Sondra Tilley. Motown was noted as a company that had interchangeable parts among their various groups. Sondra and Betty were perfect examples.

After several attempts at reforming The Velvelettes, executives at Motown decided to disband the group entirely. The Velvelettes did live on as members of The Vandellas.

Past Members:

Carolyn Gill*
Mildred Gill*
Bertha Barbee*
Norma Barbee*
Betty Kelley*
Annette McMillan
Sandra Tilley

*Original members

UPDATE *

In 1971, "These Things Will Keep Me Loving You" became a hit in the United Kingdom, peaking at number 34 on the UK charts. Despite the new success, the group did not reunite until 1984, following a rare concert appearance by the cousins and the sisters at the request of Bertha. Together the Gill sisters and Barbee cousins then went on to re-record their original hits as well as some new songs for the album *One Door Closes* for Motorcity Records. The group continues to tour today.

Three decades after the group left Motown, the company released a CD, *The Very Best of the Velvelettes* featuring 15 tracks, including four previously unreleased selections. A 19-track CD *The Velvelettes: The Best Of* was released in the UK in 2001. The 2005 *The Velvelettes: The Motown Anthology* is a double album with 48 tracks.

In 2006, the Velvelettes contributed to the double CD *Masters of Funk, Soul and Blues Present a Soulful Tale of Two Cities*. Lamont Dozier, Freda Payne , George Clinton and Bobby Taylor recorded remakes of songs from Philadelphia International Records. The Velvelettes sang "One Of a Kind Love Affair", originally recorded by The Spinners.

37. Jr. Walker & The All Stars

Autry Dewalt Walker II, or "Jr." as he is known, came to Motown Records in a roundabout way that both Walker and Motown regard as a stroke of luck.

Junior's story begins in a small club in his hometown of Battle Creek, Michigan. His saxophone style was the anchor for his band's overall sound. The other original members of the group were drummer Tony Washington, guitarist Willie Woods, and keyboardist Vic Thomas. Johnny Bristol saw Junior perform one night and encouraged him to meet with a friend, Harvey Fuqua, who had a small record company called Harvey Records. When Bristol brought Junior to Harvey Records, Fuqua saw a raw talent, who with the proper handling could be a great recording artist. Fuqua signed Junior to a three record deal, but neither Junior nor Harvey Records proved very successful. When Harvey Records folded, it was back to Battle Creek for Junior Walker. He continued to work in clubs around the area but longed for another recording contract.

It wasn't long before he received a call from his old friend Harvey Fuqua, who had surfaced with a newly formed record company in Detroit which was owned by Fuqua's brother-in-law, Berry Gordy. Fuqua informed Junior that Gordy was looking for new talent, and he wanted Junior to come to Detroit for an audition with Motown Records.

Junior recalls that first meeting with Berry Gordy: "When I got to the Motown offices, Berry and Harvey were waiting for me. Berry told me that Harvey had been singing my praises and he wanted a look for himself. He was primarily interested in singers, and a saxophone player who sang really didn't fit the image he was trying to create at Motown. As soon as Berry saw what I could do, he turned to Harvey and told him to sign me to a contract. Making that trip to Detroit was the best move I ever made in my life."

The usual procedure was followed with Junior at Motown Records. He was brought along slowly, learning all aspects of the recording business from the ground up. He was unique among the Motown stable of stars because he had his own band and wrote most of his own material. It was finally decided that Junior and his group, The All-Stars, would record a tune titled "Shotgun".

"Shotgun" broke in 1964, and Junior recalled how it changed his life forever: "I had been with Motown for about a year when I recorded "Shotgun". It wasn't till that time that I fully realized how popular the "Motown Sound" was. I was getting offers to perform all over the country. "Shotgun" also established my credibility as a recording artist."

The relationship between Motown and Walker proved to be a good one as such hits as "Roadrunner, "How Sweet It Is To Be Loved By You", "These Eyes" and "What Does It Take To Win Your Love" followed.

One of the most enjoyable aspects of working at Motown Records was the family atmosphere and the sense of friendly competition that existed among the artists. Junior explained: "We all got along very well at Motown. Whenever someone had a hit on the charts, the other groups would be pulling for them. It also meant that they would try even harder to get a bigger hit of their own. It was all very friendly competition and it benefited not only the company but the artists, as well, because we all strived to do the best we could."

It was fortunate that everyone got along so well because Motown would put quite a few of their acts on tour together. Junior recalls those days of the "Motortown Revue" fondly: "We would climb on a bus and be out on the road for very long periods of time. I really didn't mind because it gave me a chance to see a lot of the country. I never minded touring as much as some of the other acts."

Junior backstage with his saxaphone

Junior was one of the most liked artists at Motown. He never made any waves within the company and got along well with his fellow performers. His great respect for Berry Gordy accounts for his flexibility within the company. To this very day, he gives full credit to Motown for his success in the music world. "I am able to travel all over the world, playing songs that were on the Motown label. Everything I know about the business, Motown taught me."

As the 80's approached, Walker was one of the few remaining Motown originals left with the company. Junior had made the transition with Motown to California, unlike many of the Motown family members. Junior was working with producer Norman Whitfield, when it became obvious that Motown wanted to put most of its energies into other, newer artists.

Junior still enjoys great success as a concert performer all over the world. When I interviewed him, he had just returned from a European tour. One of the biggest highlights of his past Motown career was a guest appearance on the popular "Saturday Night Live" television show. More people saw Junior that night than in all of the Motown Revues combined.

Junior informed me there was no way he would ever slip into the "Whatever Happened To" category. He told me, "Just watch for me in your area, because I'M A ROADRUNNER, BABY."

An old friend visits Junior backstage in Detroit

UPDATE *

In 1979, Junior Walker went solo and was signed to Norman Whitfield's Whitfield Records label. He was not as successful as he had been with the All Stars in his Motown period. Walker also played the sax on the group Foreigner's "Urgent" in 1981. The solo was actually cobbled together from tapes that he had made with the band. He later recorded his own version of the Foreigner song. In 1983, Walker was re-signed with Motown.

Junior Walker died on November 23, 1995 in Battle Creek, Michigan of cancer at the age of 64. He had been inducted into the Rhythm and Blues Foundation that year. Drummer James Graves died in 1967 in a car accident, and guitarist Willie Woods in 1997 at age 60. Victor "Vic" Thomas died November 28, 2010 in Battle Creek , Michigan. Mr. Billy "Stix" Nicks resides in South Bend, Indiana and teaches at Notre Dame University; he is the only survivor of the band today.

Junior Walker's remains were buried in Oak Hill Cemetery, in Battle Creek, MI, under a marker with both his birth name of Autry DeWalt Mixon, Jr., and his stage name.

Walker's "Shotgun" was inducted into the Grammy Hall of Fame in 2002.

Jr. Walker & The All Stars were inducted into the Michigan Rock and Roll Legends Hall of Fame in 2007.

38. Sammy Ward

"Singing Sammy Ward" was the second male star to emerge at Motown, following close on the heels of Barrett Strong.

Sammy was well known for his flashy style of both performing and dressing which didn't score him any points with Berry Gordy. Gordy, you see, wanted his artists to appeal to a broader base of fans, and he wanted their material to be more of the crossover variety.

He recorded his songs on the Tamla label and released "Don't Take It Away" in 1961. He also was involved in the first duet recorded for Motown in Berry Gordy's plan to reach a wider audience, but his recordings with Sheri Taylor were bluesy, and Sammy wouldn't let Berry sand off all the rough edges to make it a true Motown Sound release.

Ward's appealed more to the blues fans, and he wasn't really interested in performing any crossover material. This attitude caused Ward more than one argument with Berry Gordy, but because Berry didn't have that many talented and trained performers, he continued to use Ward in his shows.

As soon as Motown had enough qualified artists to fill out an entire show, Sammy Ward was gone. He continued to perform around the Detroit area but was never a part of the eventual success Motown was to achieve.

GALA NEW YEAR'S EVE
STAGE SHOW

Starring In Person
DIRECT FROM RECORD BREAKING PARIS ENGAGEMENT
LITTLE STEVIE
WONDER

"Workout Stevie, Workout" - "Fingertips"

★★★

MARV JOHNSON
"Crying On My Pillow" - "Congratulations, You've Hurt Me Again"

★★★

THE TEMPTATIONS
"Farewell My Love" - "I Want A Love I Can See"

★★★

BILL MURRY M.C.
Top Favorite Comedian

★★★

CHOKER CAMPBELL
And His Big Orchestra

★★★

SPECIAL ADDED ATTRACTION
LIZ LANDS
"May What He Lived For, Live"

39. Mary Wells

A 1962 official portrait of Mary Wells
Photo Courtesy R. ALLEN

Mary Wells holds the distinction of being the "First Lady" of Motown from 1961 to 1964. During that period of time no one's star shone brighter than that of Mary Wells'.

She came to Motown as a 17 year old high school student with a self-written composition in her hand titled "Bye, Bye, Baby". She was encouraged to seek an audition with Berry Gordy by Motown engineer Robert Bateman, who had heard her sing. Gordy had just started Motown Records and was very much in the market for new talent.

Berry Gordy liked what he heard and saw in Mary Wells. She was a very attractive girl, which surely wouldn't hurt her marketability. Gordy had Wells enter Detroit's United Sound Studios to record the single, "Bye Bye Baby". After a reported 22 takes, Gordy signed Wells to the Motown subsidiary of his expanding record label and released the song as a single in late 1960. It eventually peaked at No 8 on the R&B chart in 1961 and later crossed over to the pop singles chart , where it peaked at number 45. Berry Gordy assigned Smokey Robinson to produce material for Mary. Smokey wrote and produced all of her material during her four year stay at Motown.

In 1962 Mary's career took off in a big way with such hits as "The One Who Really Loves You", "You Beat Me To The Punch" and "Two Lovers", all of which reached the top ten that year. The success of "You Beat Me to the Punch" helped to make Wells the first Motown star to be nominated for a Grammy Award when the song received a nod in the Best Rhythm & Blues Recording category. The single of "Two Lovers" sold more than one million copies. Mary's career was skyrocketing so was Motown's credibility as a record company. People were now becoming very much aware of this small record company in Detroit.

In 1964 Mary Wells reached what was to be the high point of her career with the release of a Smokey Robinson tune titled "My Guy". It hit number one on the charts where it remained for eleven weeks. The Smokey Robinson song became her trademark single, reaching No. 1 on the Cashbox R&B chart for seven weeks and becoming the No. 1 R&B single of the year. The song successfully crossed over to the Billboard Hot 100, where it eventually replaced Louis Armstrong's "Hello, Dolly" at No. 1, where it remained for two weeks. The song became Wells' second million-selling single. It was one of the biggest hits Motown had experienced in its brief lifetime. It was at this time that Mary began to realize what a valuable property she was.

"I was quite young when I signed with Motown and the contract I signed paid me nothing compared to the revenue my records were bringing in for the company. My contract ran out in 1964 and when another record company offered me a much more lucrative contract, I took it. I know a lot of people think I made a mistake but I am glad I made the move because I was finally paid a decent salary for my work."

Around this time, The Beatles stated that Wells was their favorite American singer, and soon she was given an invitation to open for the group during their tour of the United Kingdom, thus making her the first Motown star to perform in the UK. Wells was only one of three female singers to open for The Beatles, the others being Brenda Holloway and Jackie DeShannon. Wells made friends with all four Beatles and later released a tribute album, *Love Songs to The Beatles*, in the mid 60's.

A lot of speculation had been made about the demise of Mary's career after she left Motown. The simple fact is that she didn't receive the attention she did at Motown. Smokey Robinson worked very hard at writing great material for Mary at Motown. They also had some for the finest musicians, producers, and engineers in the music business. They all worked hard to put out a good product, and there was a special feeling that went into each recording that other companies couldn't match. This, more than anything else, led to Mary's decline in the record industry. Mary would probably, in the long run, have been better off staying at Motown for less money and making up the difference in a long and successful career. This is purely a personal opinion, mind you, but in my research I found something that backs up my theory. The next tune Mary was to have recorded was a song entitled "Where Did Our Love Go". That tune eventually was given to The Supremes and went to number one. It launched their careers from that point on.

It is a know fact around the Motown studios that it didn't really matter who would record a certain song--it was usually destined be a hit. Today(1982) Mary is on the comeback trail recording for CBS records. She plays a lot of discos and "Oldies" shows. Whenever Motown Records is mentioned, Mary Wells' name is sure to be brought up as one of the pioneers that helped put Motown on the map.

Labels:

Motown, 20th Century Fox, Atco, Jubilee, Reprise, Epic, Motorcity

UPDATE: *

In 1972, Wells scored a UK hit with a re-issue of "My Guy", which was released on the Tamla-Motown label and climbed to No. 14. Though a re-issue, Wells promoted the single heavily and appeared on the British TV show Top of The Pops for the first time. Despite this mini-revival, Wells decided to retire from music in 1974 to raise her family

In 1977, Wells divorced Cecil Womack and returned to performing. She was spotted by CBS Larkin president Larkin Arnold in 1978 and offered a contract with the CBS subsidiary, Epic Records , which released *In And Out Of Love* in October 1981. The album, which had been recorded in 1979, yielded Wells' biggest hit in years, the disco single, "Gigolo".

The song became a smash at dance clubs across the country. A 12-minute mix hit No. 13 on Billboard's Hot Dance/Club Singles chart and No. 2 on the Hot Disco Songs chart. A three-minute radio version released to R&B stations in January 1982 achieved a modest showing at No. 69. It turned out to be Wells' final chart single.

Mary Wells making magic in Detroit 1981
Photo Courtesy KATHY RYAN

Leaving CBS in 1983, she continued recording for smaller labels, gaining new success as a touring performer. In 1989, she was celebrated with a Pioneer Award from the Rhythm and Blues Foundation during its inaugural year

In 1990, Wells recorded an album for Motorcity Records , but her voice began to fail, causing the singer to visit a local hospital. Doctors diagnosed Wells with cancer . Treatments for the disease ravaged her voice, forcing her to quit her music career. Since she had no health insurance, her illness wiped out her finances, causing her to sell her home. As she struggled to continue treatment old Motown friends, including Diana Ross , Mary Wilson , members of The Temptations and Martha Reeves, made donations to support her, along with the help of admirers such as Dionne Warwick , Rod Stewart, Bruce Springsteen, Aretha Franklin and Bonnie Raitt. That same year, a benefit concert was held by fellow fan and Detroit R&B singer Anita baker . Wells was also given a tribute by friends such as Stevie Wonder and Little Richard on *The Joan Rivers Show*.

In 1991, Wells brought a multi-million dollar lawsuit against Motown for royalties she felt she had not received upon leaving Motown Records in 1964 and for loss of royalties for not promoting her songs as the company should have. Motown eventually settled the lawsuit by giving her a six-figure sum.

In the summer of 1992, Wells' cancer returned and she was rushed to the Kenneth Norris Jr. Cancer Hospital in LA. Due to the effects of her unsuccessful treatments and a weakened immune system, Wells died on July 26, 1992 at the age of 49. After her funeral, Wells was laid to rest in Glendale's Forest Lawn Memorial Park.

Though Wells has been eligible for induction into the Rock and Roll Hall of Fame- she was nominated twice in 1986 and 1987 - she has yet to achieve it. Wells earned one Grammy Award nomination during her career, and in 1999 the Grammy committee inducted Wells' "My Guy" into the Grammy Hall of Fame , assuring the song's importance. Wells was given one of the first Pioneer Awards by the Rhythm and Blues Foundation in 1989. A year later, the foundation raised more than $50,000 to help with Wells' treatment after her illness had wiped out all of her finances. In 2006, she was inducted into the Michigan Rock & Roll Legends Hall of Fame. Mary Wells' biggest hit, "My Guy", was voted a Legendary Michigan Song in 2009.

* Wikipedia

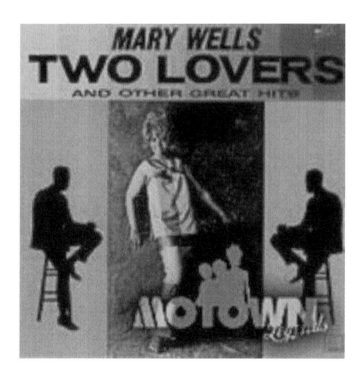

40. Kim Weston

Kim Weston started her singing career like many of the Motown stars, in a church choir. She was a pupil of the legendary James Cleveland in her early days and seemed destined to go on with her choir to great heights in the musical world.

Kim relates: "I wasn't the least bit interested in a show business career outside of my gospel singing. With my religious background a show business career was taboo. At the time I was a teenager so the whole idea seemed very remote to me".

It was a chance meeting with Motown's Eddie Holland that brought Kim to their attention. She was singing demonstration records for Johnny Thornton's record company one afternoon to earn a little money. At the session was Eddie Holland who was with Motown Records. He was so impressed with Kim's voice that he prompted Johnny to bring her by the studio to meet Berry Gordy.

Everyone at Motown was anxious to have Kim join the company but as stated earlier, her religious background was a stumbling block. After lots of soul searching and quite a bit of prompting from the song writing team of Holland, Dozier and Holland, Kim signed a Motown contract. Kim remembers her contract with mixed emotions: "I wish I would have had someone around me who had a show business background. Today a lot of young artists have good representation when they enter into a contract. Everything is explained and worked out

187

for them so they understand all facets of the contract. I was quite young when I signed my contract and at the time I thought I was being treated unfairly, but as I grew a little older I saw that other record companies were much worse in treating their performers."

Kim was one of the first female performers signed by Motown and they wanted her to be more of an up-tempo singer. She preferred to sing ballads despite having two very successful songs; "It Take Two" and "Take Me In Your Arms", that were on the upbeat side.   Motown officials felt that having Kim sing ballads slowed the shows down. At the time most of Motown's performers were doing up-tempo material.

It was at Motown that Kim met and married her husband, Mickey Stevenson. He was in charge of the Artist Development Department. Simply speaking, he was in charge of recruiting talent for the company. Kim felt that her husband was never given full credit for his contributions to Motown. "Mickey brought much of the talent into Motown that created the Motown Sound. Many people have taken credit for creating the Motown Sound but it was Mickey who recruited most of the people who developed it."

Mickey Stevenson was very creative indeed. It was he and Marvin Gaye who co-produced many of Motown's biggest hits. It was Mickey's suggestion that Marvin team up with several of the Motown female stars and record duets. That suggestion was a stroke of luck for everyone at Motown, including Kim Weston. She toured for several years with Marvin, singing not only her duets but other material as well.

Kim feels that Berry Gordy proved to be a saving grace for many of the artists who grew up in Detroit. For years such stars as Jackie Wilson, Della Reese, James Cleveland and Bill Haley all had to go elsewhere to enjoy stardom. With the advent of Motown there was a facility in Detroit that would keep home grown talent at home where they belonged. "Berry was a genius when it came to harnessing the local talent and keeping them under one roof. He saw what Detroiters had to offer and when he got the sound he was after, success followed. It's not easy to keep that sort of creativity and quality at a peak for so long but Berry did just that," Kim fondly volunteered.

Kim had a burning desire to become an actress despite notable success with records. She received permission from Motown to go to New York and study acting. She became quite proficient at acting, doing several shows in New York. She returned home hoping that Motown might expand its horizons to include theater. Unfortunately she was told that Motown was in the record business, and that she would be expected to return to the recording studio and performing aspects of the business.

It was at this time that Motown was in the process of realigning its management people. Mickey Stevenson lost a lot of his authority within the company. Kim also noticed a move within the company to give preferential treatment to certain stars. All of this left a bad taste in Kim's mouth. She offered some insights on the inner workings of a record company: "If you don't have your own producer, or someone in the company who was on your side, you could be in big trouble--your records might never get released. I was with Motown for six years and I never had more than two releases a year. I never did a solo album either. I must admit I was very disappointed, but as time went by I saw that these things are all part of the business and many companies treated their artists much worse than Motown."

When it came time for contract renewal Kim felt she wanted to get her acting career off the ground so she left Motown. She worked with Bill Cosby as well as in various stage productions, much to her delight. The theater, after all, was her first love, so she had no problem making the switch from recording.

Kim's final assessment of her Motown career is very honest and forthright. "When I was coming up in Detroit I had no one to look up to who had made it. Through Motown's help and guidance, today's kids have all of the Motown stars to emulate. We were from all sorts of backgrounds and we found success right here in our hometown. The training I received with Motown has helped me in everything I have done to this very day. It was a terrific time in my life. I will always be great full."

Today (1982) Kim is very much involved in helping Detroit youth establish themselves in the world of music and theater. She and her musical conductor Teddy Harris have a summer workshop where they share their expertise with aspiring young artists. Aside from an occasional singing engagement, Kim's workshop and charity work keep her very busy.

UPDATE: *

Along with many former Motown artists, she signed with Ivan Levine's Motorcity Records in the 1980s, releasing the single "Signal Your Intention", which peaked at #1 in the UK Hi-NRG charts. It was followed by the album *Investigate* (1990), which included some re-recordings of her Motown hits as well as new material. A second album for the label, *Talking Loud* (1992), was never released, although all the songs were included on the compilation *The Best Of Kim Weston* (1996).

Today she is a disc jockey on a local Detroit radio station, where she sponsors the summer events at Hart Plaza. She also tours sporadically, often alongside former Motown colleagues Mary Wilson, Martha Reeves and Brenda Holloway . She is also featured on the 2006 four-CD release of the Motortown Revue series.

*Wikipedia

SYREETA

Stevie's former wife Syreeta

41. Stevie Wonder

Stevie Wonder

If anyone could imagine the success a young child by the name of Steveland Morris was to enjoy at Motown Records, it would read like a fairy tale.

Steveland was born blind in Saginaw, Michigan in 1950. His background was much like most of the other Motown performers. in that he was poor and came from a rather large family. The first type of music Steveland can recall hearing was Gospel music. "When I was a small child, I can remember hearing Gospel music on the radio in our home. Steveland recalls, My mother would listen to it quite often and I would sing along."

Steveland's family moved to the Detroit area in the late fifties and settled in Black Bottom, where music was a mainstay of the people who lived there.

Steveland's uncle gave him a harmonica which he soon mastered, as well as a set of drums, which was given to him by the local Kiwanis Club. One of Steveland's friends happened to be the younger brother of Ron White of The Miracles. Steveland would sit in the White's living room and imitate their songs, much to Ron's delight. Ron White was so enthralled with the youngster that he decided to get Steveland an audition with Brian Holland, who was a Motown executive. Steveland recalls that he was totally unaware that it was an audition at all: "I was very young, maybe ten or eleven at the time, so I went into the Motown offices singing. I was having fun doing what I did everyday. I was too young to realize I was supposed to be nervous."

The Motown officials were suitably impressed with young Steveland Morris, but they had some nagging doubts about his age and the care he would need. Nonetheless, with his mother's permission, Motown became his legal guardian. Steveland signed with Motown Records and the first step was taken toward what was to become the making of a legend.

One of the first things Motown changed about Steveland Morris was his name.

Berry and Lucy Gordy, along with Billie Jean Brown, a Motown official, finally came up with "Little Stevie Wonder" as the child's new stage name. It is said that after Berry Gordy watched the youngster audition, he called him a little wonder, and the name stuck. Stevie continued in his regular school and recorded and learned instrumentation after school, which proved to be somewhat of a problem. One thing Motown officials forgot when they signed Stevie was the fact that he was just a kid. His pranks and practical jokes were almost his downfall at Motown. He would harass the secretaries, run around in the halls, and interrupt the recording sessions.

Stevie had been with Motown for almost two years before his first hit record. He had recorded the regional Detroit single, "I Call It Pretty Music, But the Old People Call It the Blues", which was released on Tamla in late 1961. Wonder released his first two albums, *The Jazz Soul of Little Stevie* and *Tribute to Uncle Ray*, in 1962 to little success. He had recorded several tunes which received some regional exposure, but it wasn't until he recorded a live tune that things really started to happen for Stevie. The title of the tune was "Fingertips" and it was such a crowd pleaser that the orchestra and Stevie continued to play the song in a different key. The finished product was "Fingertips-Parts I & II".

Stevie with Clarence Paul at the Walled Lake Casino doing 'Fingertips'
Photo Courtesy T. COX

By 1963, both the single and the album from which it came were number one on the Billboard charts, a first for the Billboard rating system. As Stevie's success continued, his studies faltered, to the point where his teachers encouraged him to give up music. "My teachers told me that I needed to give more time to my studies. I was encouraged to give up my music until

I got my studies back in check. Eventually Motown hired a tutor for me and we were able to get my studies back where they should be."

A lot of people thought Stevie was unsupervised at Motown, but nothing was further from the truth. Clarence Paul, Stevie's mentor, looked after him like a father. All of the Gordy family treated him like a son, as did all of the Motown performers and musicians. The fact was, Stevie had a company full of supervision and he was raised with more love and attention than a lot of youngsters were.

A rather unfortunate circumstance occurred to Stevie that occurs to most fourteen year olds--his voice was changing. After his first hit of "Fingertips", it was quite a while before Stevie hit the charts again. That was in 1964 and without proper material none of Stevie's tunes were released that year. Rumors were heard around the Motown offices that Stevie might have seen his greatest success and it might be time to drop him from the roster of talent. It was at this time that Stevie became very interested in writing, and with the help of Sylvia Moy, a member of the Motown writing staff, wrote a tune titled "Uptight". This tune re-established Stevie as a hit maker in good standing with Motown.

In 1968 Stevie recorded an album of instrumental soul/jazz tracks, mostly harmonica solos, under the pseudonym (and title)*Eivets Rednow*, which is "Stevie Wonder" spelled backwards. The album failed to get much attention, and its only single, a cover of "Alfie", only reached number 66 on the U.S. Pop charts and number 11 on the U.S. Adult Contemporary charts.

Stevie followed "Uptight" with such hits as "Blowing In The Wind", "A Place In The Sun", and "I Was Made To Love Her" just to name a few.

By now, Stevie Wonder was seventeen years old and anything but little. He was six feet tall and loaded with talent, energy, and enthusiasm.

From 1967 through 1970 Stevie continued to build his reputation as a first rate live performer, a reputation he had gained as an eleven year old headliner and show stealer on many Motown shows. He was becoming a legitimate Motown star, rather than a unique, Shirley Temple type entertainer, not exactly an easy feat, considering the stable of talent Motown had at the time. Such tunes as "For Once In My Life", "My Cherie Amour" and "Signed, Sealed, And Delivered, I'm Yours", gave his public a new view of the former child star. He was maturing into a very talented man and his work reflected the change.

One major change in Stevie's life was his marriage to Syreeta Wright, a young Motown hopeful, whom Stevie met and fell in love with during some recording sessions. Even though that marriage didn't last, it marked a new direction in Stevie's life, and Motown didn't necessarily agree with it. Motown had a program for success that wasn't to be questioned. Unfortunately, in Stevie's case, they were dealing with a highly creative individual who liked to experiment.

The rift became so wide that when Stevie turned twenty one, he asked for, and was granted a release from his Motown contract.

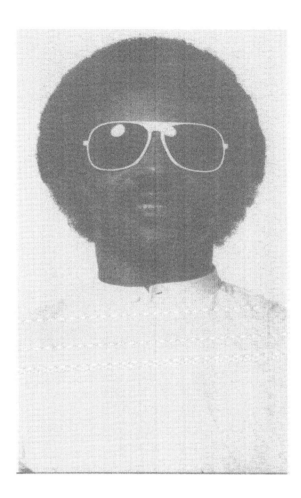

As guardians for Stevie, Motown held back a portion of his earnings until his twenty-first birthday. Motown had moved out to California by this time and Stevie went with them. With the money Stevie was given, he opened a recording studio, where he was free to experiment to his heart's content. Speaking on his departure from Motown, Stevie had this recollection: "I realize that commercialism is very important to record sales, but not at the expense of originality. They both must be in some sort of balance. I felt my originality would also be commercially successful."

This chapter has a happy ending. Stevie took a two year hiatus from Motown and learned to play the Arp and Moog Synthesizer, which were quite unusual instruments at the time. During this period he also recorded a tremendous amount of material for future use. In 1972 Stevie resigned with Motown Records for an unheard of thirteen million dollars for seven years. Also included in the deal was for Stevie to have artistic control over his material, as well as his own production company.

With the great success Stevie and Motown have enjoyed in the last decade, the money seems to be well spent.

Update

Released in late 1972, *Talking Back* featured the No. 1 hit "Superstition", which is one of the most distinctive and famous examples of the sound of the Hohner clavinet keyboard. The song features a rocking groove that garnered Wonder an additional audience on rock radio stations. *Talking Book* also featured "You are the Sunshine of My Life", which also peaked at No. 1. During the same time as the album's release, Stevie Wonder began touring with the Rolling Stones to alleviate the negative effects from pigeon-holing as a result of being an R&B artist in America. Wonder's touring with The Rolling Stones was also a factor behind the success of both "Superstition" and "You Are the Sunshine of My Life". Between them, the two songs won three Grammy Awards.

Innervisions, released in 1973, featured "Higher Ground"(#4) as well as "Living For The City" (#8) Both songs reached No. 1 on the R&B charts. Popular ballads such as "Golden Lady" and "All in Love Is Fair" were also present, in a mixture of moods that held together as a unified whole. *Innervisions* generated three more Grammy Awards, including Album 0f The Year . The album is ranked #23 on *Rolling Stone Magazine's* 500 Greatest Albums of All Time. Wonder had become the most influential and acclaimed black musician of the early 1970s.

On August 6, 1973, Wonder was in a serious automobile accident while on tour in North Carolina , when a car in which he was riding rear-ended a flatbed truck, sliding under the back of the truck and causing the bed of the truck to crash through the car's windshield, striking Wonder in the head. This accident left him in a coma for four days and resulted in a partial loss of his sense of smell and a temporary loss of sense of taste, as Wonder was to tell reporters later.

Despite the setback, Wonder recovered all of his musical faculties, and re-appeared in concert at New York's Madison Square Garden in March 1974 with a performance that highlighted both up-tempo material and long, building improvisations on mid-tempo songs such as "Living For The City".

By 1975, in his 25th year, Stevie Wonder had won two consecutive Grammy Awards-- in 1974 for *Innervisions* and in 1975 for *Fulfillingness' First Finale*.

The double album with extra EP *Songs In The Key Of Life*, was released in September 1976. According to critics on both sides of the Atlantic it was sprawling in style, unlimited in ambition, and sometimes lyrically difficult to fathom. The album was hard for some listeners to assimilate, yet is regarded by many as Wonder's crowning achievement and one of the most recognizable and accomplished albums in pop music history. The album became the first of an American artist to debut straight at #1 in the *Billboard* charts, where it remained for 14 non-consecutive weeks. Two tracks became #1 Pop/R&B hits, "I Wish " and "Sir Duke". The baby-celebratory "Isn't She Lovely" was written about his newborn daughter Aisha, while songs such as "Love's in Need of Love Today" (which years later Wonder would perform at the post-September 11,2011 *America: A Tribute To Heroes* telethon) and "Village Ghetto Land" reflected a far more pensive mood. *Songs in the Key of Life* won Album of the Year and two other Grammys. The album ranks 56th on *Rolling Stone Magazine*'s 500 Greatest Albums of All Time .

After a nearly three-year break Stevie thought it might be time to think about going back into the studio. Wonder did return, and recorded the soundtrack album *Journey Through The Secret Life Of Plants*(1979), featured in the film The Secret Life of Plants . Mostly instrumental, the album was composed using the Computer Music Melodeon, an early sampler.

Hotter Than July (1980) became Wonder's first platinum-selling single album, and its single "Happy Birthday " was a successful vehicle for his campaign to establish Dr. Martin Luther King's birthday as a national holiday.

In 1982, Wonder released a retrospective of his '70s work with *Stevie Wonder's Original Musiquarium.* Wonder also gained a #1 hit that year in collaboration with Paul McCartney in their paean to racial harmony, "Ebony and Ivory".

1984 saw the release of Wonder's soundtrack album for *The Woman in Red* . The lead single, "I Just Called to Say I Love You ", was a #1 pop and R&B hit in both the United States and the United Kingdom , where it was placed 13th in the list of best-selling singles in the UK published in 2002. It went on to win an Academy Award for "Best Song" in 1985.

On July 2, 2005, Wonder performed in The Live 8 concert in Philadelphia .

Wonder's first new album in ten years, *A Time To Love* , was released on October 18, 2005, after having been pushed back from first a May and then a June release. The album was released electronically on September 27, 2005, exclusively on Apple's iTunes Music Store. The first single, "So What the Fuss", was released in April. A second single, "From the Bottom of My Heart" was a hit on adult-contemporary R&B radio. The album also featured a duet with India.Arie on the title track "A Time to Love".

Wonder performed at the pre-game show for Super Bowl XL in Detroit in early 2006, singing various hit singles (with his four-year-old son on drums) and accompanying Aretha Franklin during "The Star Spangled Banner ".

On August 28, 2008 Wonder performed at the Democratic National Convention in Denver , Colorado. Songs included a previously unreleased song, "Fear Can't Put Dreams to Sleep," and "Signed, Sealed, and Delivered, I'm Yours".

On February 23, 2009, Wonder became the second recipient of the Library of Congress's Gershwin Prize for pop music, and honored by President Barack Obama at the White House.

On July 7, 2009, Wonder performed "Never Dreamed You'd Leave In Summer " and "They Won't Go When I Go" at the Staples Center for Michael Jackson's memorial service. On October 29, 2009, Wonder performed at the 25th anniversary concert for the Rock and Roll Hall Of Fame . Among performing songs with B.B. King , Wonder performed Michael Jackson's 'The Way You Make Me Feel", during which he became emotionally distraught and was unable to perform until he regained his composure.

On March 6, 2010, Wonder was awarded the Commander of the Arts and Letters by French Culture Minister Frederic Mitterrand . Wonder had been due to receive this award in 1981, but scheduling problems prevented this from happening. A lifetime achievement award was also given to Wonder on the same day, at France's biggest music awards.

In February 2011, the Apollo Theater announced that Stevie Wonder will be the next in line for the Apollo Legends Hall of Fame. The theater said that the singer will be inducted into the New York City institution's Hall of Fame in five months.

42. Writers of Motown

With all of the wonderful sounds that were produced at Motown Records, I felt I owed those writers, who produced that music, a chapter of their own.
I tried to present a good cross section of writers who wrote for Motown. To those writers I have omitted, I apologize.

With that in mind, I present- The Motown Writers Chapter!

SMOKEY ROBINSON

In the early days of the Motown Record Company, Berry Gordy wrote a lot of his own music. Many of the performers who were signed to Motown in those early days were quite creative and brought their own material with them.

One of the first such artists was William "Smokey" Robinson. When Berry and Smokey met, Berry was primarily interested in Robinson as a performer, but he found out that Smokey was quite a prolific songwriter. Smokey wrote the first hit song Motown had called "Shop Around" which his group The Miracles, recorded. When Berry Gordy saw Smokey's ability to write songs, he had Robinson work with the various new artists who were arriving daily at the Motown studio.

One of the first stars Smokey worked with was Mary Wells. Mary was a young singer who came to Motown loaded with potential. With Smokey Robinson's material she was able to reach her greatest success. Two of her biggest hits were "Two Lovers" and "My Guy," which went to number one in 1963.

One of the reasons many Motown insiders ascribe to Mary's failure when she left Motown was the lack of Smokey Robinson material. When Mary left, Smokey worked with several of the other female performers, such as Brenda Holloway and Kim Weston, for whom he produced some very good material, especially "When I'm Gone" for Brenda Holloway.

Smokey was particularly adept at writing love songs, and this explanation by Smokey might give you some insight as to why: "Everyone has experienced love, be it either joyful or painful. I think it really strikes a cord with the listening audience because they can identify with that feeling."

Lest you think that Smokey Robinson wrote only love songs, let me introduce you to The Temptations. Berry Gordy was searching for the right material for his five-man group and eventually he called on his ace songwriter, Smokey Robinson, to work with the group. In the following three years Robinson produced such hits as "It's Growing", "Getting Ready", "I'll Be In Trouble", "The Way You Do The Things You Do" and The Temptations' first number one hit, "My Girl". You must keep in mind that during this period, Smokey either wrote or co-wrote such songs as "I'll Be Dog-Gone" for Marvin Gaye, "First I Look At The Purse" for The Contours, and of course, most of the material for his group, The Miracles.

Smokey Robinson was a rare individual in the early days of Motown. He wrote constantly, writing more than 1,000 songs in his career. He wrote material and produced music for any and all who needed his help. Smokey related to me in a recent interview, "I always try to tailor-make songs for the various artists. I will try to fit the song to the singer and with that in mind, I've had some very good fortune with my work." Everyone who has enjoyed a Smokey Robinson song is equally grateful for his success.

HOLLAND-DOZIER-HOLLAND

The names of Eddie Holland, Lamont Dozier, and Brian Holland are found on so many Motown Records that I could fill a page listing the titles. It would be an understatement to say that the Holland, Dozier, Holland writing team was successful at Motown. What is interesting about all three is that they came to the company as singers.

Eddie Holland had a very big hit, titled, "Jamie", in 1961. That's when his brother Brian came to the company. Berry Gordy inquired as to whether Brian would like to come to the company as a singer and Brian agreed. His singing career was short- lived though, due to his shyness, but he stayed on as a a writer, which was his first love. When Motown merged with Anna Records in the early 60's, Lamont Dozier came along with several artists, but before long he found his niche in the songwriting field. Working as writers for Motown didn't pay as much in those early days, just $2.50 per week, plus royalties from future record sales. I know this sounds like very little money, but you must remember Berry Gordy would use their material when other companies wouldn't let them in the door.

Brian Holland recalls that the team of Holland, Dozier, Holland had their first hit record with a Martha and The Vandellas tune titled, "Come And Get These Memories": "We wrote that tune back in 1963 and Berry felt it would be a good song for Martha and her group. They were on a tour with Marvin Gaye at the time, but Berry felt so strongly about the song, he had them fly home for a recording session. "Come And Get These Memories" was the first big hit for Holland, Dozier, Holland as well as for Martha And The Vandellas."

The Holland, Dozier, Holland songwriting team used love as a basis for most of their tunes, both content and title. "Baby Love", Stop In The Name Of Love", and "You Can't Hurry Love" were perfect examples of the number one hits they wrote with love as a central theme.

A lot of people have come to the conclusion that The Supremes were the only group to benefit from Holland, Dozier, Holland material, but such was not the case. They wrote "Can I Get A Witness" and "How Sweet It Is" for Marvin Gaye. For The Four Tops they wrote "I Can't Help Myself", and "Baby I Need Your Lovin' "among others. Smokey Robinson was the beneficiary of "Mickey's Monkey" and the list goes on and on.

One thing people don't realize is that most songs were recorded by several groups. All of the records were sent to a quality control meeting where they in turn would give their recommendations to Berry Gordy as to who had the strongest version of the song. Brian Holland recalls those meetings with Berry Gordy: "Once a week, we would meet to decide which material would be released. Berry would listen to everyone's opinion very carefully, but the final decision was his to make and he would inevitably release the strongest material. He was correct about 90% of the time, so you can see why Motown was as successful as it was."

With the success Motown was having, the need for quality material vastly increased. Berry Gordy instituted competitions between his writing teams and the result was some fantastic music. The Holland, Dozier, Holland team saw this competition as a perfect time to expand their horizons. They began to mix their writing style to encompass jazz, classical, rhythm and blues, and contemporary. A perfect example of their innovations can be heard in their number one hit, "I Hear A Symphony", for The Supremes.

The success of Motown and that of the Holland, Dozier, Holland songwriting team were almost unparalleled in the 1960's. As the 60's drew to a close, Eddie, Lamont and Brian decided it would be in their best interest to open a record company of their own. There had been some growing disenchantment with their royalties and some fringe benefits which never materialized, so the trio left Motown to form Invictus Records.

One of the groups signed by Invictus was The Chairman Of The Board which had a hit record with "Give Me Just A Little More Time". That type of success was rare for the trio and before long Lamont Dozier left Invictus to perform, as well as produce other artists. In the legacy they left behind at Motown, the names and music of Eddie Holland, Lamont Dozier, and Brian Holland will live forever.

Discography (Courtesy Wikipedia)

Production

Year	Song title	Original artists	Covering artists
1962	"Dearest One"	Lamont Dozier	
	"Old Love (Let's Try It Again)"	Mary Wells	Martha and the Vandellas, Four Tops
	"Darling, I Hum Our Song"	Eddie Holland	Martha and the Vandellas, Four Tops
1963	"Leaving Here"	Eddie Holland	Motörhead, Lars Frederiksen and the Bastards, Pearl Jam, The Birds, The Who, Brownsville Station, The Messengers, The Rationals, and The Volts
	"Locking Up My Heart"	The Marvelettes	
	"What Goes Up Must Come Down" / "Come on Home"	Holland & Dozier	
	"Tie a String Around Your Finger"	The Marvelettes	
	"Come and Get These Memories" / "Jealous Lover"	Martha and the Vandellas	Hattie Littles, Anna King, The Supremes
	"You Lost the Sweetest Boy"	Mary Wells	Dusty Springfield
	"(Love Is Like a) Heat Wave" / "A Love Like Yours (Don't Come Knocking Everyday)"	Martha and the Vandellas	The Who, Linda Ronstadt and The Jam / Dusty Springfield, Juice Newton, Ike & Tina Turner and The Animals, Phil Collins
	"(He Won't Be True) Little Girl Blue"	The Marvelettes	
	"Mickey's Monkey"	The Miracles	Martha and the Vandellas, The Hollies
	"Too Hurt to Cry, Too Much in Love to Say Goodbye" / "Come on Home"	The Marvelettes & The Andantes (credited as *The Darnells*.)	The Supremes
	"When the Lovelight Starts Shining Through His Eyes" / "Standing at the Crossroads of Love"	The Supremes	Dusty Springfield and The Zombies

"I Gotta Dance to Keep From Crying"	The Miracles	
"Quicksand" / "Darling I Hum Our Song"	Martha and the Vandellas	
"Live Wire" / "Old Love (Let's Try It Again)"	Martha and the Vandellas	
"Run, Run, Run" / "I'm Giving You Your Freedom"	The Supremes	
"Can I Get a Witness"	Marvin Gaye	Dusty Springfield, The Rolling Stones, Sam Brown, The Steampacket, Lee Michaels, The Temptations, The Supremes
1964 "A Tear from a Woman's Eyes" (non-single release; competed with "The Way You Do The Things You Do" for a spot on The Temptations' 7th single.)	The Temptations	
"My Lady Bug Stay Away from That Beatle" (never released)	R. Dean Taylor	
"Like a Nightmare" / "If You Were Mine"	The Andantes	
"In My Lonely Room"	Martha and the Vandellas	The Supremes, The Action
"Just Ain't Enough Love"	Eddie Holland	
"Where Did Our Love Go"	The Supremes	Adam Ant, Soft Cell, Pussycat Dolls, Three Ounces of Love, The J. Geils Band, Donnie Elbert, The Manhattan Transfer
"Baby Don't You Do It"	Marvin Gaye	Small Faces, The Who, The Black Crowes, The Band
"Guarantee for a Lifetime" (never released)	Mary Wells	
"Baby I Need Your Loving" / "Call on Me"	Four Tops	Johnny Rivers. Eric Carmen, and Joe Stubbs / Shorty Long
"Candy to Me" /	Eddie Holland	/

"If You Don't Want My Love"		Martha and the Vandellas, Four Tops
"Whisper You Love Me Boy" (never released)	Mary Wells	The Supremes, Chris Clark
"Baby Love" / "Ask Any Girl"	The Supremes	
"Come See About Me" / "(You're Gone But) Always in My Heart"	The Supremes	The Afghan Whigs, Barbara Mason, Jr. Walker & the All Stars, Choker Campbell and Pat Lewis
"Without the One You Love (Life's Not Worth While)" / "Love has Gone"	Four Tops	
"You're a Wonderful One"	Marvin Gaye	Don Bryant
"How Sweet It Is (To Be Loved by You)"	Marvin Gaye	Jr. Walker & the All-Stars, The Elgins, James Taylor, Grateful Dead, and Liz Lands
1965 "Where Did You Go"	Four Tops	
"Stop! In the Name of Love" / "I'm in Love Again"	The Supremes	The Hollies, Talas, Kim Weston, Jonell Mosser
"You've Been a Long Time Coming"	Marvin Gaye	
"Who Could Ever Doubt My Love" (non-single release; album-track only)	Brenda Holloway	The Supremes, The Isley Brothers
"Nowhere to Run"	Martha and the Vandellas	Hattie Littles, The Messengers, Tower of Power
"Back in My Arms Again" / "Whisper You Love Me Boy"	The Supremes	
"I Can't Help Myself (Sugar Pie, Honey Bunch)"	Four Tops	Gloria Lynne, Bonnie Pointer, Robert Parker, Johnny Rivers, and Axe
"The Only Time I'm Happy" (limited promo-only single release)	The Supremes	
"Mother Dear" (cancelled single release) / "He Holds His Own"	The Supremes	

"Nothing but Heartaches" / "He Holds His Own"	The Supremes	
"Love (Makes Me Do Foolish Things)"	Martha and the Vandellas	
"It's the Same Old Song" / "Your Love Is Amazing"	Four Tops	KC and the Sunshine Band and Joe Stubbs
"Mother Dear" (cancelled single release) / "Who Could Ever Doubt My Love"	The Supremes	
"I Hear a Symphony" / "Who Could Ever Doubt My Love"	The Supremes	Stevie Wonder, The Isley Brothers and The Temptations
"Something About You"	Four Tops	Sisters Love
"Take Me In Your Arms (Rock Me a Little While)"	Eddie Holland	The Isley Brothers, Kim Weston, Mother Earth, Jermaine Jackson, The Doobie Brothers, and Blood, Sweat & Tears
"Darling Baby"	The Elgins	
"There's a Ghost in My House"	R. Dean Taylor	The Fall
1966 "(I'm a) Roadrunner"	Jr. Walker & the All-Stars	Fleetwood Mac, Steppenwolf, Peter Frampton, James Taylor, and Jerry Garcia
"This Old Heart of Mine (Is Weak for You)"	The Isley Brothers	The Supremes, Ronald Isley, Rod Stewart, Tammi Terrell and The Contours
"Ask any Man"	Tony Martin	
"My World Is Empty Without You"	The Supremes	Mary Wilson, The Afghan Whigs
"Put Yourself in My Place"	The Elgins	
"There's No Love Left"	The Isley Brothers	
"Shake Me, Wake Me (When It's Over)" / "Just as Long as You Need Me"	Four Tops	The Hollies
"Helpless" / "A Love Like Yours (Don't Come	Kim Weston	

Knocking Everyday)"

"Call on Me"	Shorty Long	
"Love Is Like an Itching in My Heart" / "He's All I Got"	The Supremes	
"Who Could Ever Doubt My Love"	The Isley Brothers	
"I Like Everything About You"	Four Tops	
"I Guess I'll Always Love You"	The Isley Brothers	The Supremes
"Nothing but Soul"	Jr. Walker & the All-Stars	
"Love's Gone Bad" / "Put Yourself in My Place"	Chris Clark	
"You Can't Hurry Love" / "Put Yourself in My Place"	The Supremes	Phil Collins, Stray Cats, Dixie Chicks
"Little Darling (I Need You)"	Marvin Gaye	
"Reach Out I'll Be There" / "Until You Love Someone"	Four Tops	Diana Ross, Michael Bolton, Gloria Gaynor, Bobby Taylor & the Vancouvers and Snuff
"Stay in My Lonely Arms"	The Elgins	
"You Keep Me Hangin' On" / "I Wanna Mother You, Smother You with Love" (cancelled single release)	The Supremes	
"You Keep Me Hangin' On" / "Remove This Doubt"	The Supremes	Vanilla Fudge, Rod Stewart, Kim Wilde, Rose Banks, Wilson Pickett, Reba McEntire, Mary Wilson
"Standing in the Shadows of Love" / "Since You've Been Gone"	Four Tops	The Jackson 5, Joe Stubbs, Rod Stewart, Barry White and Snuff
"I'm Ready for Love"	Martha and the Vandellas	The Temptations
"(Come 'Round Here) I'm the One You Need"	The Miracles	The Jackson 5, The Cowsills, The GP's

	"Heaven Must Have Sent You"	The Elgins	Bonnie Pointer
1967	"Just One Last Look" (non-single release; album-track only)	Four Tops	The Temptations
	"Love Is Here and Now You're Gone" / "There's No Stopping Us Now"	The Supremes	Michael Jackson
	"Your Love Is Amazing"	Shorty Long	
	"Jimmy Mack" / "Third Finger, Left Hand"	Martha and the Vandellas	James Brown, Laura Nyro, Bettye LaVette
	"Bernadette" / "I Got a Feeling"	Four Tops	
	"My World Is Empty Without You"	Barbara McNair	
	"The Happening" / "All I Know About You"	The Supremes	
	"Just Ain't Enough Love"	The Isley Brothers	
	"7-Rooms of Gloom" / "I'll Turn to Stone"	Four Tops	Blondie
	"I Understand My Man"	The Elgins	
	"Your Unchanging Love" / "I'll Take Care of You"	Marvin Gaye	
	"Reflections" / "Going Down for the Third Time"	Diana Ross & the Supremes	Syreeta, Four Tops, The Temptations, Michael McDonald, Sweet, Luther Vandross
	"One Way Out"	Martha and the Vandellas	
	"You Keep Me Running Away" / "If You Don't Want My Love"	Four Tops	
	"I Got a Feeling"	Barbara Randolph	
	"In and Out of Love" / "I Guess I'll Always Love You"	Diana Ross & the Supremes	
1968	"Whisper You Love Me Boy"	Chris Clark	

	"Forever Came Today"	Diana Ross & the Supremes	The Jackson 5
	"I'm in a Different World"	Four Tops	
1969	"We've Got a Way Out Love"	The Originals	
	"Crumbs off the Table" (H–D–H as "Edythe Wayne")	The Glass House	Laura Lee
1970	"Give Me Just a Little More Time" (H–D–H as "Edythe Wayne")	Chairmen of the Board	Kylie Minogue
	"(You've Got Me) Dangling on a String" (H–D–H as "Edythe Wayne")	Chairmen of the Board	
	"Band of Gold" (H–D–H as "Edythe Wayne")	Freda Payne	Sylvester, Charly McClain, Belinda Carlisle, Bonnie Tyler and Kimberley Locke
	"Westbound #9" (H–D–H as "Edythe Wayne")	The Flaming Ember	
1972	"The Day I Found Myself" (H–D–H as "Edythe Wayne")	Honey Cone	
	"Don't Leave Me Starvin' For Your Love"	Holland-Dozier-Holland	Laura Lee
	"Why Can't We Be Lovers"	Holland-Dozier-Holland	

SYLVIA MOY

Sylvia Moy had the distinction of being one of the few female writers and producers Motown had in their employ.

Sylvia attended college at Wayne State University in Detroit, and dreamed of a career as a singer. After working at various clubs around Detroit, the natural progression was to seek a record contract, so she visited all of the record companies in the Detroit area. Whenever she interviewed at a record company, would inquire if she had any original material to sing. After a few of these letdowns, Sylvia decided to write some material of her own, but as she recalls, she met with a great deal of resistance: "Most of the record companies just didn't understand my material. I met with very little success until Marvin Gaye and Mickey Stephenson told me to come over to Motown and speak with Berry Gordy. When I went to the office and began to sing my material, everybody joined in with me. They were beating out the beat on the desk and for the first time I felt that someone understood me."

Berry gave Sylvia a job as a staff writer and she was assigned to work on material for various artists. Her first major success, co-written with Stevie Wonder, was "Uptight". Stevie's career was at a low point at this time due to a change in his voice. The writers were unable to come up with the right material for him, but with Sylvia Moy's help, "Uptight" became a huge hit and Stevie's career was back on track.

Sylvia co-wrote several other tunes with Stevie, such as "With A Child's Heart", "Shoo-Be-Do-Be-Do-Dum-Day" and one of Stevie's biggest hits, "My Cherie Amour".

Martha and The Vandellas were also the beneficiaries of two of Sylvia Moy's tunes which did quite well, "My Baby Loves Me" and "Honey Chile". In 1971 when Motown decided to move to California, Sylvia Moy elected to stay in the Detroit area and produce material.

When Motown left, it took a little bit of Sylvia Moy with it. She relates her feelings about her former employers: "There was a special loyalty and love involved with Motown. Even though it's been nearly 12 years since we went our separate ways, I still feel that love."

ASHFORD & SIMPSON

ASHFORD & SIMPSON

Most of the entertainment world knows Nick Ashford and Val Simpson as a superstar recording duo, but few realize that they received one of their first show business breaks as a songwriting team at Motown Records. When the Motown officials heard their fresh new material, they were offered jobs as staff writers.

Most of the material they wrote was used on various albums by several groups. This was rewarding, but not in the financial sense. It wasn't until Marvin Gaye and Tammi Terrell recorded "Ain't No Mountain High Enough" in 1967 that people began to take notice of Ashford and Simpson. Berry Gordy was quite impressed with the duo and not long after the Gaye-Terrell release of "Ain't No Mountain High Enough", he decided he would like Nick and Val to concentrate their efforts on material for Diana Ross. Berry was in the process of designing a solo career for Diana, and he knew she would need new material. Gordy was convinced that Ashford and Simpson could provide that material and with the release of "Reach Out And Touch Somebody's Hand", Diana's first solo hit, his faith in the team was rewarded.

"Reach Out" has become the highlight song of Diana Ross' show, and provided the avenue for her solo career. It was another Ashford and Simpson tune which provided Diana with her first number one hit as a solo artist. "Ain't No Mountain High Enough", which was a big hit for Marvin Gaye and Tammi Terrell several years earlier, was re-recorded with new orchestration and production techniques, giving the tune new life. Diana still uses this tune as the opening song in her show, with great success. One last Ashford and Simpson tune was recorded by Diana Ross in 1971 titled "Remember Me" that reached the top 20.

Unfortunately for Motown, Nick Ashford and Val Simpson had their eyes on greener pastures-- a singing career of their own. Today, the song writing duo are superstar performers in their own right, and are singing, as well as writing their own material.

In recent times, Ashford & Simpson have recorded and toured sporadically. In 1996, they opened the restaurant and live entertainment venue Sugar Bar in New York City, which has an open mic on Thursday nights where performers have included Queen Latifah and Felicia Collins. They recorded the album *Been Found* with poet Maya Angelou in 1996. Around this time, they were also featured disc jockeys on New York's KISS-FM radio station.

The duo continues to write and score today. They are given writing credit on Amy Winehouse's 2007 CD *Back to Black* for the single "Tears Dry On Their Own". The track is based on a sample of Marvin Gaye and Tammi Terrell's 1967 Motown classic hit "Ain't No Mountain High Enough". They have started performing their live act in intimate spaces such as Feinstein's at the Regency in New York and the Rrazz Room in San Francisco, and in January 2009, they released a CD and DVD of their live performances entitled *The Real Thing*. On June 22, 2009 they made a guest performance at a party at Tribeca Rooftop, New York, to celebrate Virgin Atlantic's Birthday party. They also made their first appearance in Tokyo, Japan and performed eight shows in four days at Blue Note Tokyo in November 2009.

Sadly Nick Ashford died after battling throat cancer in August 2011 at his home in New York City.

43. Pilots Of The Airwaves

After writing all of the chapters on the various stars that recorded or worked for Motown Records, I feel I must add a chapter on the disc jockeys who worked in the Detroit area during the Motown era.

These people could make or break a record quite easily on their airwaves, so I think their recollections are a valid addition to this book. You will discover that some of these disc jockeys were very instrumental in the careers of many Motown stars.

I must apologize to the many disc jockeys around the country that were just as influential as the Detroit based jocks. Due to a shortage of time, I was able only to contact the disc jockeys who worked in the Detroit market during Motown's rise to fame. With that in mind I present:

THE PILOTS OF THE AIRWAVES

ROBIN SEYMOUR

Robin Seymour

If there was a granddaddy of rock disc jockeys in the Detroit area, it would have to be Robin Seymour. Robin began his career as a rock disc jockey at WKMH radio in Dearborn, Michigan. Robin had been working at the station for some time, under various formats, but then rock and roll music became the rage. Robin was one of the first to join the rock parade.

In the late fifties, Robin met a young man by the name of Berry Gordy, who had been producing some very fine music independently. He had written some material for Jackie Wilson and Marv Johnson that brought him some recognition in the record industry. Robin Seymour set up a meeting between Berry Gordy and some record executives that would have given Gordy his own label. Robin explains, "Murray Duetch and Lucky Karl of Pure International Publishing wanted to meet Berry and set him up in his own label. I arranged a meeting with Berry at the Statler Hotel in Detroit and much to everyone's surprise, Berry turned down the offer, saying he wanted to try it on his own first. He eventually started his own label and called it Motown Records." When Berry started releasing records on the Motown label, Robin Seymour was one of the first to play his tunes. Robin's audience liked the freshness of the Motown music and especially the fact that it was coming out of their home town of Detroit. Robin Seymour's popularity grew to the extent that CKLW television in Windsor, Canada, offered him a weekly television show titled "Teen Town".

Teen Town was a sort of local American Bandstand and it gave a lot of exposure to the Motown acts. Robin recalls what part the Motown acts played in this new venue back in 1964: "I needed new guests every week and Berry Gordy would always be glad to send his various acts over to the show. We were a big help to each other in those early days. I gave some of the Motown acts their first television exposure."

It was in 1964 that Robin left WKMH (by this time WKNR) radio and went to work for the legendary radio station CKLW. His television show was now called "Swinging Time", and it was a must-stop for all major national acts who were passing through the Detroit area. The Motown artists continued to be a mainstay on the "Swinging Time Show". Swinging' Time featured 50 to 75 local kids dancing six days a week to the top billboard hits. Each show, two teens were chosen to offer "yea" or "boo" opinions on new records. The 30-minute weekday shows were broadcast live, and the hour-long Saturday show was taped early in the day and aired at 3 pm. As a matter of fact, Robin recalls the reaction the viewers would have if a Motown group didn't play the show regularly. "We would get all kinds of calls inquiring when a certain Motown group would be on the show. That's the type of impact there artists had on the community."

As the seventies approached, the Motown Sound was entering its second decade, but Robin Seymour left the broadcasting business for private industry. Today, Robin Seymour is involved in the direct sales of oil paintings at the San Marcos Galleries in Berkley Michigan. (1982) He is also a frequent speaker at sales training seminars for many companies. As he relates, "I've always been involved in the communications industry and now I'm communicating at a different level."

UPDATE: In 1970, Seymour recreated his WKMH "Bobbin' with the Robin" show for *Cruisin' 1956*, part of a CD series of Top 40 radio re-creations conceived and produced by Ron Jacobs.

Seymour left both broadcasting and Detroit in the late '70s and moved to the Los Angeles area where he owns a successful video production company.

MARC AVERY

Marc Avery

Marc Avery arrived in Detroit in 1961 and went to work for WJBK radio. It wasn't long before Marc established himself as one of Detroit's top morning disc jockeys, working the 6 - 10 A.M. slot at WJBK. Marc, like most of the area disc jockeys, worked a lot of the sock hops around town. This is where he first encountered most of the Motown acts. Berry Gordy saw to it that his acts were always available to the jocks for their hops.

Marc recalls three young women who were especially eager to promote their record: "Three young ladies named The Supremes were always willing to work any hop I hosted. They weren't having much success with their records, but they would join me any time I requested, and I would always play their records. I remember they must have released ten flops in a row and then one day, we got in a Supreme record titled, "Where Did Our Love Go?" and the rest is history."

Every Tuesday was record promotion day at WJBK and all the representatives and their artists would come to WJBK to promote their new records. When Marc Avery left the air at 10A. M., a small boy would be waiting for him on the WJBK steps. Marc would take him to those meetings because he was quite interested in getting into the music business. His name was Stevie Wonder, and you may have heard the name once or twice.

Of all the disc jockeys I interviewed for this book, only Marc Avery recorded a song for Motown. Marc relates how it came about: "One day while I was the Motown offices, Berry inquired if I would sing a rather unusual song he had. It was an answer song to "Big Bad John", the Jimmy Dean hit. The title was "Small Sad Sam", and I had Martha and The Vandellas backing me up on the record. It was a flop, but I am proud to say I recorded a song for Motown."

Today (1982) Marc Avery works for radio station WCZY-FM in Detroit and is quite involved with the St Jude Children's Hospital Charity. He hosts a yearly golf tournament, with the proceeds earmarked for St. Jude's.

TOM SHANNON

Tom Shannon

Tom Shannon is probably best recognized for his radio show on CKLW in Windsor, Ontario. Windsor is located directly across the Detroit River, so the sounds of Motown were a mainstay of the CKLW programming.

Tom's first association with the Motown Sound came in his hometown of Buffalo, New York, where he was working in the early sixties. "I was working at a station that played a lot of the Miracles and Temptations tunes. Berry Gordy sent both groups to Buffalo to make some personal appearances and I got to meet them for the first time. When I went to work at CKLW, our friendships grew all the more. "

Shortly after Tom arrived in Detroit, he was invited to the annual Motown Christmas Party where he met all the Motown acts. His friendship with Berry Gordy became quite evident when Berry asked Tom to emcee the prestigious Motown Revue at Detroit's Fox Theater. The revue ran for a week, between Christmas and New Year's Day each year, and played to overflow crowds. Only the top celebrities in Detroit were involved, from the emcee to the closing act.

With the Motown Sound sweeping the country, Tom Shannon explains his thoughts on why it was so popular. "Berry Gordy came up with the right sound at the right time. He had a black sound that was very appealing to the white audiences and for the first time they not only listened, they bought." As Tom became more involved in the Detroit area, he noticed the hometown pride that existed due to Motown and its influence. "When listeners would call me to request a certain song, they would refer to the various artists by their first names. It was like they were personal friends. That's how close the fans felt to Motown, and all of its artists."

Disc jockeys from around the country envied their counterparts in Detroit, having the Motown acts at their disposal. When Tom Shannon moved on to do several television shows in Detroit, the friendships he had established at Motown proved to be a big asset. "The Motown acts were always available for guest appearances on my shows. The Temptations, Stevie Wonder, The Miracles, and Martha and The Vandellas, were just a few of the acts who appeared for me. We were all great friends and I'm quite pleased to be able to say that."

Tom has some rather interesting closing overviews of his association with the Motown scene. "It was quite exciting to be around and see Motown take off as it did. I will always be grateful that I was a little part of it. "

TOM SHERMAN

Tom Sherman

Tom Sherman hosts a weekly nostalgia show on radio station WCHB in Inkster, Michigan (1982). Tom's input was important to this chapter for several reasons. First, he was raised in Boston, and could give me a view of Motown that I couldn't get from a Detroiter. Secondly, he toured various military installations with several Motown groups, when he was working for Armed Forces Radio. Lastly, he is one of the most knowledgeable people on the Motown Sound I know.

Tom's first recollection of the Motown Sound came as a teenager back in Boston, where the sounds of Jackie Wilson and The Miracles were starting to be heard on the Boston airwaves. Berry Gordy was producing these artists independently and leasing the recordings to various record companies. Tom explained how he came to hear the latest Motown offerings firsthand: "I had relatives in Detroit and I would visit every summer. Ernie Durham was a very popular disc jockey in Detroit and he played a lot of Motown music. When I would go back to Boston, my cousins would tape the Ernie Durham show and send it to me in Boston. I would get some of the Motown tunes before the record stores in town."

When Tom arrived back home in Boston after his stint with Armed Forces Radio in Germany, he went to work for WBZ radio. This was in 1963 and the Motown Sound was beginning its big push across the nation, and in Boston the record stores were being deluged with requests for any and all Motown music.

People of all races were clamoring for Motown music, so much so in fact, what white customers would go to the black record stores to find the Motown releases. Tom explains how the white listening audiences affected the black music industry: "In the early days of rock and roll, black music was considered "Race Music" and rarely, if ever, played on white stations. When Motown's artists started having their music accepted by white audiences, the "Race Music" label wouldn't do. It was at this time that the term "Soul Music" came into vogue and it was mainly due to Motown Records."

"Blacks all over the country took great pride in the Motown Sound. It gave blacks a great sense of pride to see black acts appearing on the top television shows and in major nightclubs," recalls Sherman. "Wherever you were around the country, people would seem to envy you if you were from Detroit; it was as if you were an extension of Motown Records."

Tom Sherman sums up his feelings on the Motown Sound in this fashion: "Berry Gordy was in the right place, with the right sound, at the right time. His music was new and fresh and he presented it in a truly theatrical manner. If Berry Gordy had brought his music along any sooner, no one would have listened. If he had come along any later, he would have been following a trend, instead of leading one."

DAVE SHAFER

Dave Schafer

226

When Dave Shafer came to Detroit from Arizona in the early 60's he took over one of the most popular radio shows in the Detroit radio market. Dave became "Jack, The Bellboy" at WJBK radio in Detroit, which was one of the most prestigious radio shows in the country.

At that time major record companies would break their new records on stations in Detroit, New York, and Philadelphia because of their listening audiences. It was entirely possible for a record company to know if they had a hit record by the requests the stations got overnight. When Dave worked as Jack The Bellboy, quite a few records were broken on his show and quite a few were sent to the WJBK offices by Berry Gordy at Motown Records. "Berry was always available to the disc jockeys. He would have us over to the Motown studios regularly, to hear new releases and to meet the various artists. We used many of the Motown artists on sock hops we would emcee in the Detroit area, so it was important we have a good relationship."

Dave had a good relationship with quite a few of the Motown artists, but one young man who had recorded a tune titled "Contract On Love" has a special place in Dave Shafer's heart. "I played a tune titled, "Contract On Love", by a youngster named Stevie Wonder one night on my show. A few minutes later I received a call from Stevie thanking me for playing the record. I put him on the air so my listeners could talk to him and I got a great response. Stevie would call back on a regular basis and it became a bit on my show. He would be a guest disc jockey and answer fan's questions. You could see even at that age, he was a terrific talent."

Dave Shafer left WJBK and moved on to CKLW, where he served as the morning man for eight years. While at CKLW, Dave enjoyed his greatest success. His show ranked number two in the very competitive Detroit market. Working mornings gave Dave an opportunity to do a lot more sock hops around the Detroit area. "I remember picking up Stevie Wonder and The Supremes at their homes to take them to entertain at sock hops. They were still teenagers at the time and didn't have a ride in many cases. Another group that I remember fondly was The Spinners. They would show up on their own at various dances I would be at and perform free of charge. I am real happy for the success they're enjoying today. They worked very hard to get where they are."

Eventually, Dave Shafer left the Detroit radio market to work in the management end of the business. He served in many management capacities in several out-of-state radio markets. Today, Dave Shafer is a top executive at WCZY-FM in Detroit. Many of the disc jockeys who worked for him at WCZY are old friends from his days in the Detroit market. Dave Shafer started out as Jack The Bellboy, but he wound up running the place.

DICK PURTAN

Dick Purtan

Dick Purtan came to work in the Detroit area in 1965 when he started for WKNR in Dearborn, Michigan. He worked the 10PM to 1 AM shift at the station in those early days, and one song he claims will always be associated with his move to Detroit was sung by The Four Tops, "I Can't Help Myself". "This song was very popular at the time my family moved to Detroit. For some reason I have always associated that song with my working in the Detroit area, "Dick relates.

Working 10 PM to 1AM at WKNR, Purtan had a call-in line titled "Pick and Play". Purtan recalled many Motown songs being requested on his show. "Motown artists were very popular and a great number of my listeners would call to request their favorite records."

Purtan moved to the early drive time slot where has remained for virtually all of his fifteen-odd years in Detroit, working at WXYZ and CKLW, where he can be heard today. (1982) Purtan does recall, however, that Motown music was equally popular in Buffalo and Cincinnati where he worked prior to his arrival in Detroit: "When I worked in other towns, Motown music was just as popular as it was in Detroit. It was a universally popular sound that everyone could enjoy."

Today, Dick Purtan is one of the most popular disc jockeys on the Detroit airwaves. He can be heard on numerous commercials and has hosted his own television special. Dick has become quite a celebrity in the Detroit area and a pleasant addition to this chapter on Motown era jocks.

UPDATE :

After more than four decades on the air, Dick Purtan retired in 2010 to the dismay of the entire city of Detroit. This two time inductee to the Radio Hall of Fame and fixture in charity fund raising (his efforts for The Salvation Army have yielded in excess of $ 24 million dollars) has been listening to the clamoring of fans and in June of 2011 went back on the air with a podcast which can be heard at www.dickpurtan.com on Friday.

HANK O'NEIL

Hank O'Neil has worked off and on in the Detroit market since 1959, when he joined radio station WEXL. In the early 1960's, WEXL began playing rock and roll exclusively, and part of their programming was coming from within the Detroit area. Motown Records was in its earliest beginnings at this point, with such acts as The Miracles, Mary Wells, and The Marvellettes starting to get quite a bit of air play.

Hank O'Neil remembers another of those early Motown groups fondly: "I used to host quite a few sock hops at Notre Dame High School, on Detroit's east side. We used to have various recording artists come in to promote their records. This particular night we were to have The Contours appear with us. They were popular due to a song titled,

"Do You Love Me", which was climbing the charts like crazy. When word got out we were having The Contours, over 1,700 kids showed up."

From WEXL, Hank moved around to various radio stations in and out of the Detroit market. At one time Hank worked in the Washington D.C.- Baltimore area, where there was a great deal of interest in the Motown performers. As a matter of fact, when Motown wanted to test-market a record, it was released in the Washington D.C.-Baltimore market.

While working in Washington, Hank O'Neil hosted several concerts which featured many Motown acts at an outdoor area called Echo Park. This was to be the last such involvement O'Neil would have with Motown acts until he went to work for radio station WHND in Detroit. "Honey Radio", as it is known, has the only all oldies format in the Detroit area. (1982)

Hank O'Neil explains why the Motown Sound remains such an integral part of WHND's programming: "When Berry Gordy produced his original Motown music, it had something very attractive for all listeners. Today, with our oldies format at Honey Radio, we are able to relive those special Motown sounds on a regular basis, as though time had stood still. It is by far the most requested type of music we play at the station."

An interesting sidelight to Honey Radio and Motown is that The Contours, The Latin Counts, and The Marvelettes, (all former Motown groups) appear regularly at WHND sponsored shows around the Detroit area.

Honey Radio gave these acts some of their first exposure when they reformed. Today at WHND radio in Detroit, the Motown Sound is alive and well, thanks to their oldies format.

Update

Hank O'Neil passed away on January 8, 2011 after a short illness.

"FRANTIC" ERNIE DURHAM

Ernie Durham

"Frantic" Ernie Durham began his Detroit area radio career at WJLB in 1959, and soon established himself as a master of the rhymed phrase. His rapid-fire phraseology became a standard for disc jockeys all over the Detroit area. Being a disc jockey, Ernie knew many recording artists who resided in Detroit and the surrounding areas.

Jackie Wilson was one of those friends, and he introduced Ernie to a young record producer by the name of Berry Gordy. Ernie recalls that first meeting with Berry Gordy: "Berry had been doing some independent record producing at the United Sound Studio in Detroit. He explained to me that his goal was to get his own label and produce local talent. The more I listened the more I believed he could do it."

The first meeting was to be the beginning of a long relationship between Ernie Durham and the Motown recording people. While Ernie hosted a teen dance at the Twenty Grand Nightclub each week, all of the Motown acts appeared to perform their latest material. As a matter of fact, Ernie's dances became a "must stop" for entertainers who were in Detroit to promote their records.

Frantic Ernie Durham

Of all the Motown groups Ernie came to know from his radio show, one group in particular proved to be the most popular on WJLB. Ernie relates: "Whenever we got requests on our switchboard, it would invariably be for a Supremes song. No one caught the imagination of our listeners like The Supremes did. They were a success story all of Detroit could identify with."

 Ernie Durham's show was a launching pad for many Motown acts and their records. It was not unusual to have over 50% of the WJLB programming set up with Motown music.   Ernie gives his theory as to why Motown Records became a success: "It was a unique situation for Motown Records. They were being produced locally by a Detroiter who was using local talent. Nowhere in the country were more successful recording stars being produced than in Detroit. It was a story in itself."

In the early 70's "Frantic" Ernie Durham left WJLB to enter private business. It wasn't until 1982 that Ernie was lured back to the airwaves at WQBH in Detroit. Ernie hosts a weekly nostalgia show on Saturdays from ten to two where his familiar rhymed patter is once again pleasing many listeners.

Update: Durham later went to work at WJLB's successor, WQBH, and also at WJR in Detroit. In 1992, he returned to the airwaves to host a Saturday night R&B oldies show on another Detroit station, WDET-FM. He died December 2 of that year after suffering from chest pains.

Berry Gordy recorded his first records
and his first hits at United Sound Studios

The Motown Museum

Motown Historical Museum is one of Detroit's most popular tourist destinations. Each year, the museum attracts thousands of visitors from across the nation and around the globe. The museum was founded in 1985 by Ester Gordy Edwards. Its mission is to preserve the legacy of Motown Record Corporation and to educate and motivate people, especially youth, through exhibitions and programs that
promote the values of vision, creativity and entrepreneurship.

Motown Historical Museum
2648 W. Grand Boulevard
Detroit, Michigan 48208

(313) 875-2264

Ms. Esther Gordy Edwards passed away after a long illness on August 24, 2011. She will be missed by generations of artists and fans who love Motown as she did.

Jack Ryan

About The Author

Jack Ryan, like The Motown Sound, was born and raised in Detroit, Michigan. Growing up with such a dynamic musical influence as The Motown Sound around him, Jack, like many others during the 60's became quite a fan of Berry Gordy's new sound.

While writing for such publications as City Magazine, The Dearborn Times Herald, The Observer and Eccentric and most recently C&G Publications, where he served as chief entertainment writer, Jack had the opportunity to interview many of the Motown recording artists. It was during these interviews that Jack decided he would compile the interesting material he had gathered into book form.

"Recollections" is the product of a years work which saw Jack Ryan interview virtually everyone connected with Motown Records. The stories found in "Recollections" are an account of the Motown era by the stars and behind the scenes personnel who made the hits.

That is why "Recollections" is such a unique view of The Motown Sound. Jack Ryan still lives in the Detroit area with his wife, Kathy.

Update:

Since the publication of "Recollections", Jack Ryan has travelled many roads in the entertainment industry. He has worked in television as an entertainment reporter. He has also contributed to his wife, Kath's weekly radio show as a movie reviewer.

Concert promoter and booking agent followed but for 28 years, Jack has managed former Motown recording artists, The Contours.

18803820R00132

Made in the USA
Lexington, KY
25 November 2012